Praise for Morris Berman

"Ecstasy, witchcraft, bewilderment—these ten loving vignettes on scandalous corners of Russian culture, by one of our most seasoned cultural critics, are a tribute to imperishable art even in our catastrophic time."

—Caryl Emerson, Professor Emerita of Slavic Languages and Literatures, Princeton University

The Soul of Russia

Also by Morris Berman

Social Change and Scientific Organization

TRILOGY ON HUMAN CONSCIOUSNESS:

The Reenchantment of the World

Coming to Our Senses

Wandering God: A Study in Nomadic Spirituality

TRILOGY ON THE AMERICAN EMPIRE:

The Twilight of American Culture

Dark Ages America: The Final Phase of Empire

Why America Failed: The Roots of Imperial Decline

A Question of Values (essays)

Destiny (fiction)

Counting Blessings (poetry)

Spinning Straw Into Gold (memoir)

The Man Without Qualities (fiction)

Are We There Yet? (essays)

Neurotic Beauty: An Outsider Looks at Japan

Genio: The Story of Italian Genius

The Heart of the Matter (fiction)

Eminent Post-Victorians

Healing: The Defining Root of Our Existence

The Soul of Russia

From Pushkin to Tarkovsky

Morris Berman

Published by Echo Point Books & Media
Brattleboro, Vermont
www.EchoPointBooks.com

All rights reserved.
Neither this work nor any portions thereof may be reproduced, stored in a retrieval system, or transmitted in any capacity without written permission from the publisher.

Copyright © 2023 by Morris Berman

The Soul of Russia
ISBN: 978-1-64837-362-6 (casebound)
         978-1-64837-363-3 (paperback)

Interior design by Jeffrey P. Fisher

Cover design by Kaitlyn Whitaker

Cover images *(clockwise from top left)*:
Portrait of Alexander Puskin by Vasily Tropinin,
  courtesy of Wikimedia;
Portrait of Mikhail Yurievich Lermontov by Pyotr Zabolotsky,
  courtesy of Wikimedia;
Andrei Tarkovsky at Festival de Cannes, 1972,
  photographer unknown

The Greek god Apollo stands for order, clarity, and logic—the rational mind—whereas his counterpart, Dionysus, represents disorder, emotion, and ecstasy; the irrational mind. Nietzsche believed that the optimal state of human consciousness was an integration of the two. [Author commentary]

[O]pposing forces routinely coexist in biological systems.

—Bessel van der Kolk, *The Body Keeps the Score*

Acknowledgments

As in the past, I want to thank John Trotter for his efforts in selecting and preparing the illustrations used in this book, and to Jeffrey P. Fisher for his work in layout and design. In this case, I wish to add Chuck Jines to the list, for the time he put in helping me search and select the photographs. I couldn't have done any of this without them.

Contents

List of Illustrations	xiii
Note to the Reader	xv
Preface	xvii
1. Pushkin: The Queen of Spades	1
2. Gogol: The Nose	11
3. Lermontov: The Soul of a Cossack	21
4. Mussorgsky: Pictures at an Exhibition	27
5. Chekhov: The Siren	33
6. Bely	41
7. Diaghilev & Co.: Les Ballets Russes	49
8. Stravinsky: The Rite of Spring	61
9. Bulgakov: The Master and Margarita	75
10. Tarkovsky: Solaris	81
Notes	89
About the Author	103

List of Illustrations

1. Alexander Pushkin, by Vasily Tropinin, 1827
2. Nikolai Gogol, daguerreotype by Sergei Lvovich Levitsky, 1845
3. Mikhail Lermontov, by Peter Zabolotsky, 1837
4. Mikhail Lermontov, *View of Tiflis*, 1837
5. Modest Mussorgsky, artist unknown, 1874
6. Anton Chekhov, by V. Chekhovskii, 1889
7. Andrei Bely. Photographer and date unknown
8. Sergei Diaghilev, photo by J. de Streletsky, 1910
9. Igor Stravinsky, ca. 1920-25; photographer unknown
10. Mikhail Bulgakov, 1928; photographer unknown
11. Andrei Tarkovsky. Photographer and date unknown

As for photo credits: all are in the public domain except for Tarkovsky, #11. A good faith effort was made to locate the source or owner, without success. If any reader can provide that information, I shall be happy to insert it into future editions of this book. In the case of Bely, #7, I need to state the provenance as lichnosti.net.

Note to the Reader

Perhaps unlike any of my previous books, there is something deeply personal about this one. I explored my relationship to Russian culture in an essay I wrote years ago called "My Russia" (included in the collection *Are We There Yet?*), in which I discussed my early exposure to Lermontov and Mussorgsky, and the Cossack context of my family history. Before immigrating to America, my family lived in *shtetls* like the ones pictured in the paintings of Marc Chagall. As a college student studying Russian as a second language, I read Pushkin's "Queen of Spades," Gogol's "Nose," and Lermontov's *Hero of Our Time* in the original versions, before reading them in English. (This may have also been the case with Chekhov's "Siren," although I can't be sure.) And over the years, I read Andrei Bely's *Petersburg* no less than three times, and Bulgakov's *Master and Margarita* twice (both in English). Nor did I ever fully recover from Tolstoy's "Death of Ivan Ilyich," or the Grand Inquisitor section of Dostoevsky's

Brothers Karamazov. In addition, the theme of alternative realities, which is strongly present in most of the portraits sketched in this book, forms a major part of my own academic work, starting with *The Reenchantment of the World* in 1981. As I say at the end of "My Russia," this is a world that, culturally speaking, I know in my bones. I offer all this not as any Apologia Pro Vita Sua, but as an honest admission of who I am and how this book came to be. Somehow, it seemed important to me to say all this, and I also thought it might possibly be helpful to you, the reader.

At one point I thought of calling this book *Blini: A Few Tasty Bites*, because these sketches are quite brief, and hardly comprehensive. I am not an expert in Russian history, and these portraits are only intended to give the reader the flavor of each individual's achievement. They are meant to be cameos, not extended biographies, in other words. That being said, I hope you will, in fact, find them "tasty."

For the purpose of these sketches, I need to say a few words about the definition of "Dionysian" (see epigraph, above). As used in this book, the term does not always mean ecstatic, but does always mean irrational, which can include ecstatic consciousness. There is nothing, for example, ecstatic about a man losing his nose (Chapter 2), although it is certainly an irrational/surreal event. In addition, the two experiences can occasionally overlap, as they do in the story about the queen of spades (Chapter 1). So the reader should be aware that "Dionysian" here ultimately refers to alternative realities, some of which are ecstatic, and some of which are not. I hope that will not be too confusing.

Preface
The Golden Age and Beyond

The Soul of Russia is the third volume in what I call my "cameo" series: portraits of exceptional human beings. Volume One is about the Italians: *Genio: The Story of Italian Genius*. Volume Two deals with the British in the first half of the twentieth century: *Eminent Post-Victorians*. And now, closest to my heart, as already indicated, we have the Russians. *Bozhe moi* (my God!), what can one say about the Russians? That no other country in the world produced a collection of talent such as they did? That their creative work is a feast for the mind, and the senses? That their work teaches us what it means to be a human being? Yes, all of that, for sure, and I leave it to the reader to decide which aspect speaks most poignantly to him or her.

As for my own selection process in this work: talk about a challenge! Some of these authors' collected works take up entire library shelves. The Kindle edition of Chekhov's literary output, to take just one example, amounts to 6,800 pages. The published (print) version of Mikhail Bulgakov's collected works—eight volumes—runs to nearly 6,000. And so on. Following up on what I said above, any attempt to be comprehensive was out of the question. Given the fame of these individuals, "comprehensive" has been done many times over, and by eminent experts in the field. I chose, instead, to focus on texts and works that spoke to me personally.

That was one part of it. The other part was the fact that I was tracking on a theme relevant to a fair amount of the creative work done in Russia during its so-called Golden Age (most of the nineteenth century): the mixture, or attempted integration, of Apollonian and Dionysian modes of being. This heady elixir, this "dialogue" between the rational and the irrational, proved to be a kind of magic formula, in terms of creative output. Perhaps Caryl Emerson, the premier American scholar of Russian literature, put it best when she wrote that the nineteenth century witnessed a "phenomenal flowering" of Russian creativity. Even "phenomenal" doesn't quite capture it.(1)

Magical, yes; formulaic, no. It was fairly spontaneous; there was no "school" or methodology involved. However, it did have a basis, one that runs very deep in Russian history. I am referring to the folkloric tradition, which is rooted in a peasant-shamanic heritage, suffused with superstition, magic, alternative realities, and often, primal energy. For Russian scholars, it has been a major area of study; bibliographies of the subject could fill a warehouse. Indeed, millions of Russians regard this as the "true" Russia, and almost all of them are aware of it as a powerful cultural and historical undercurrent. "Scratch a Russian and you will find a Tatar," quipped Napoleon. A few decades later, the Canon of St. Paul's wrote that the sense of the supernatural permeated Russian life "more completely than that of any other of the Western nations." And more recently Suzanne Massie, in *Land of the Firebird*, had this to say:

> Told over and over again by nurses and grandmothers from time immemorial, these beloved tales of the people were the inexhaustible well of imagination from which Russian artists in the nineteenth and early twentieth centuries were to draw their inspiration. The colorful themes, the rhythms and sounds of these tales found their way into the poems of Pushkin, the stories of Gogol, and the work of scores of other Russian writers.(2)

Similarly, Orlando Figes, in *Natasha's Dance*, asserts that much Russian literature was rooted in oral narrative traditions, and that it was this that gave it its strength and originality. A good number of the greats drew on folklore in many of their works.(3) This persisted into the twentieth century, by which time European artists were finding inspiration in the primitive energy of native cultures. To many in the so-called Modernist period, writes Professor Emerson, the Dionysian element in Russian consciousness was alive and well. Andrei Bely's novel *Petersburg* (see Chapter 6) is soaking in a "hallucinating Dionysian subconscious," alternating between a rational and an intuitive response to the world, while Bulgakov's *Master and Margarita* (see Chapter 9) is filled with miracles, madness, magic, and other assorted supernatural events. All of these works, including those written or composed during the Soviet era, right down to Tarkovsky's film *Solaris* (1972), are clear examples of this particular tradition or world view, namely the notion of reality as being labile, potentially nonrational. What these writers and artists are asserting is that rational analysis or understanding is "stalked" by the nonrational, which is never very far from the surface. As Nietzsche put it in *The Birth of Tragedy*, "Men of philosophical disposition are known for their constant premonition that our everyday reality...is an illusion, hiding another, totally different kind of reality." The reader will thus forgive me if the thesis I am arguing here is, to employ the American idiom, a bit of a slam dunk.(4)

Using this as a criterion, however, would seem to leave some curious gaps in this survey of Russian creativity. Any such survey would be expected to include, at least for the nineteenth century, Dostoevsky, Tolstoy, Turgenev, and Goncharov (the author of *Oblomov*). The problem is that these men were largely realists; their focus was on social reform, for example; themes such as witchcraft or Dionysian ecstasy don't appear in their work. Dostoevsky's real talent was in human psychology; Tolstoy was searching for a "true" Christianity, as well as the levers of social reform; Turgenev, also interested in social reform, was an agnostic; and Goncharov was exploring what it meant for someone to spend their life on a couch. All of this made for great literature, but falls outside the purview of my own (not all that idiosyncratic) concerns. It does require us to note, however, that the Apollo-Dionysus dialectic is not the only source of great creativity, which is also true of much of the creativity of the twentieth century (Akhmatova, Pasternak, et al.). Nor is this dialectic the exclusive province of Russian art or literature, quite obviously.(5)

Despite much darkness in her history, Russia has been a place where the soul takes flight; and her essential gift to the West, and to the world at large, is *vibrancy*—precisely that which makes life worth living. Who could ask for more?

M.B.

Mexico City, 2023

Chapter 1

Pushkin: The Queen of Spades

What wonders they are, her old tales! Every one is a poem.

—Alexander Pushkin, in a letter to his brother, 1824, referring to his nanny, Arina Rodionovna

[It is] the pinnacle of the art of the fantastic.

—Dostoevsky, in a letter to a friend, 1880, referring to *The Queen of Spades*

The Soul of Russia

1. Alexander Pushkin

In Russia, "Pushkin" is just another name for God. He is regarded as the country's greatest poet and the founder of modern Russian literature. It was as though everything he wrote, and he wrote quite a bit, was a masterpiece: *Eugene Onegin, Boris Godunov, Ruslan and Ludmila, The Bronze Horseman,* and *The Captain's Daughter*, along with numerous short stories and collections of fairy tales. His use of the language, his idiosyncratic style, influenced many other writers, including Gorky, Turgenev, Tolstoy, and Lermontov. In a word, with Pushkin, Russian literature took a quantum leap, and was never the same again.

And all of this in a very short time, for Pushkin died in 1837, at the age of 37, being killed in a duel. He was born into the Russian nobility, and raised by a household serf, Arina Rodionovna, who was his principal source of peasant lore and the Russian folk tradition. Pushkin was the first Russian poet to pay serious attention to the folktale; *skazka*, in Russian. In fact, his works are soaking in this nonrational element, often in very creative and playful ways. In *Ruslan and Ludmila* (1820), for example, Ludmila is abducted by an evil dwarf, after which we are entertained by the magic of wizards. There is a resurrection from the dead, a magic sword and hat, and a giant talking head. In 1828, Pushkin went off to the Caucasus, where he devoted himself to transcribing the folklore of the region. Thanks to Arina's influence, Pushkin was fascinated by the fantastic stories and supernatural beliefs of southern Russia for all of his adult life. In *The Bronze Horseman* (1833), a poor young man curses the famous statue of Peter the Great, which then comes to life and hounds him to death.(1)

My favorite example of Pushkin's preoccupation with this alternative tradition is what is perhaps his best-known short story, *The Queen of Spades*, published in 1834.(2) It's fairly representative of how his mind worked, and his general outlook on the nature of reality—a creative integration of the natural, the supernatural, and the psychological. The action takes place in St. Petersburg in the 1830s, then Russia's capital. The story centers around an officer in the Army Engineers named Hermann, who is obsessed with obtaining wealth. He goes to various card games, but refrains from gambling for fear of losing what he already has. And yet, says Pushkin, "he had the soul of a gambler." Up to this point, his participation was vicarious; "he would sit up all night at the card tables, trembling feverishly, as he followed the shifting fortunes of the play." This notion of "fever" is one that runs through the entire tale.

In the course of one particular game, a man named Paul (Pavel) Tomsky tells the story of how his grandmother, the Countess Anna Fedotovna, lost a large amount of money playing faro in Paris, to the Duke of Orleans, when she was a young, attractive woman. She was at a loss of what to do, because she had no way of paying the debt; but she had a connection with the famous (or infamous) Count de St. Germain, a man renowned for his supposed knowledge of the occult arts. According to Tomsky, she approached him, and the Count gave her the secret to winning at the game. She returned to the card table, and to the Duke (this time in Versailles), followed the Count's instructions, and recouped everything she had lost.

The narration of this tale was the moment that sealed Hermann's fate, because it offered the possibility of acquiring wealth without risk—a possibility he was not able to ignore. The Countess was still alive; she was eighty-seven years old. Might there be a way he could obtain an audience with her, and persuade her to give him the secret of the Count de St. Germain? It was like medieval possession: he could think of nothing else. When he slept, says Pushkin, "he dreamed of cards, a green table, heaps of banknotes, and piles of gold coins." It seems fair to call this money-fever a form of Dionysian ecstasy. It certainly wasn't rational.

In any case, he couldn't just go up to the Countess and introduce himself; this was simply not done. However, the Countess had a ward by the name of Lizaveta, a more or less pretty girl, and Hermann effectively set about stalking her. He would stand outside her window, staring up at her as she worked on her embroidery. It was an extended campaign, but eventually he wore her down, and through a clandestine exchange of notes fired her romantic imagination. When he sent her a note asking for a rendezvous, she immediately rejected the invitation, but finally gave in to her bourgeoning desire. (Apparently Dionysus was stalking her as well.) This took the form of sending back a note outlining the layout of the Countess' house, the location of her room, and instructions as to how to find it. "That will be your opportunity to see me alone," she wrote him.

It was late at night when Hermann set out to follow her instructions—up to a point. First, he waited for the Countess' carriage to return to the house, and when it did, "an involuntary excitement seized him." Then, when she was finally settled in her room, rather than go there, he entered the room of the Countess, who was visibly shocked at the sight of this strange man. "Don't be afraid," he told her; "I have no intention of doing you harm." He proceeded to explain his purpose in confronting her, namely, to obtain the secret of the cards. But the Countess sat there stone-faced; she wouldn't reply, even as his pleading became increasingly desperate. His patience finally exhausted, Hermann took out his pistol. The Countess began to tremble, then rolled onto her back and remained motionless. She had died of fright.

The funeral was held three days later, and out of fear of some sort of divine retribution, Hermann decided to attend, and beg forgiveness from her corpse. When he bent over her dead body, it seemed to him that she winked at him. He was badly shaken, and collapsed; other mourners had to help him up. That night, over dinner in an out-of-the-way inn, he got very drunk, staggered home, and collapsed again, this time on his bed. Just before 3 a.m. he awoke. The door to his bedroom opened, and a woman in a white dress entered, and glided right up to him. It was the Countess, or more precisely, her ghost. She told him that she had been "commanded" to grant his request. By whom, Pushkin doesn't say. "The three, the seven, and the ace," she tells him, "will win for you in sequence." And with that, she turned and left the room.

Well, talk about obsession. "The three, seven, and ace haunted him in dreams," wrote Pushkin, "assuming every sort of guise…All his thoughts merged into one—to make use of the secret which had cost him so dear." As chance would have it, a famous Moscow gambling club had recently arrived in St. Petersburg. Its leader, one Chekalinsky, was "a most respectable-looking man of about sixty; he had a silvery-grey head of hair; his plump, fresh face was a picture of good nature; his eyes shone, animated by a perpetual smile." A mutual friend introduced Hermann to him, and Chekalinksky welcomed him to the card table. After watching the play for a short while, Hermann asked to place a bet. "How much?" asked Chekalinsky. "Forty-seven thousand rubles," said Hermann. A hush fell over the room. No one, Chekalinsky informed him, had ever staked more than 275 rubles on a single card. But Hermann was unfazed, and he bet the three, as the Countess had advised him. Three it was, and he walked away with a huge pile of banknotes. Hermann drank a glass of lemonade, and left.

The game was still running the next day, when Hermann returned and bet his 47,000 plus yesterday's winnings on the seven. The entire room gasped, as once again, Hermann had the winning card. On the third evening, everyone was waiting for him. No one placed a bet; everyone crowded around the table to observe the play. Chekalinsky's hands shook as he dealt the cards. Hermann bet the ace, triumphantly declaring that he had won. But no, said Chekalinsky; look, your card is the queen of spades. You have lost.

Hermann gave a violent start: Chekalinsky was right. Instead of an ace, there lay the queen of spades. At that point the queen, whose face resembled that of the Countess, winked at him, and grinned. "The old woman!" cried Hermann, in horror. He had lost it all.

The denouement: Hermann went mad, and was put away in a nearby mental hospital, where he muttered to himself, over and over again, every day, all day long, "three, seven, ace; three, seven, queen." He never returned to sanity; this was the condition in which he died, several years later.

What to make of this remarkable, peculiar story? Pushkin leaves the question open, and in its wake, numerous interpretations arose, ones that are still with us to this day. The central debate: Is this a tale of the supernatural, or is it a study in basic human (including deviant) psychology? To me, it seems obvious that it is both, at least from a Dionysian perspective, which can have aspects of a dramatic departure from ordinary reality, and aspects of obsession, mental fever. I don't believe that what occurred can be dismissed as a case of mental hallucination, because the Countess' ghost did give Hermann the correct winning numbers—ones that worked in the real, rational world (until the very end). The psychological aspect, on the other hand, which could include the mental hallucination theory, can also be seen in behavior that Pushkin depicts as "feverish": Hermann's drunken pursuit of money, as well as Lizaveta's heady desire for love—obsessions that contain strong ecstatic elements. This, I think Pushkin is telling us, is woven into the human condition, as hysterical or irrational as it may be. It is Dionysus who often drives us, rather than Apollo. And the message that the supernatural aspect has for us is that reality cannot be trusted; it is often not what it seems to be—a Russian theme, as already noted, that lasts down to Andrei Tarkovsky's film of 1972, *Solaris* (see Chapter 10), which is, like *The Queen of Spades*, both challenging and disturbing.(3)

"In the end," writes Pushkin biographer T.J. Binyon, "it is difficult not to suspect that the story is a paradox, uniting two mutually contradictory views: the literary equivalent of those prints by Escher that conflate two mutually contradictory perspectives." Pushkin, he concludes, was being deliberately tongue-in-cheek. This take on the story also has its advocates.(4)

Much of Pushkin's work, however, is based on forays into the more intense or ecstatic aspect of the Dionysian mode, typically associated with the Russian peasantry and/or the tribal peoples on the Eastern Frontier, who were regarded as exotic, or even wild. *The Prisoner of the Caucasus* (1822), for example, is a narrative poem about a Russian officer who goes in search of this primal "otherness," is captured by Circassian tribesmen, and is then saved by a beautiful Circassian woman. It is one of Pushkin's most famous works, projecting an image of the Caucasus as free, untamed, a healthy refuge from the stiffness of Russian society. This "noble savage" motif became an inspiration to a whole generation of writers, Lermontov in particular (see Chapter 3).(5)

Pushkin, then, embraced a wide spectrum, from winking playing cards to dazzling, native young maidens. In the process, he redid the spectrum of Russian literature. Both stories (among many others) have endured and are woven into the fabric of Russian culture. Russian audiences, for example, greatly enjoyed the comedy film of 1966, *Kidnapping, Caucasian Style*, in which a young anthropology student arrives in the Caucasus to study the local customs, falls in love with a girl whose uncle has arranged to have her kidnapped and married off to a rich man, and then convinces the student that the kidnapping is just part of the local folklore(!). It all sounds a bit like the Soviet version of the popular

British "Carry On" series that was running at around the same time, in which confusion leads to pandemonium. As for *The Queen of Spades*, Tchaikovsky made it into an opera, Peter Lorre starred in a radio version of it, and numerous films were based on it. What else is there to say, except that Pushkin is alive and well?(6)

Chapter 2

Gogol: The Nose

Perfect nonsense goes on in the world. Sometimes there is no plausibility at all.

—Nikolai Gogol, "The Nose"

2. Nikolai Gogol

Gogol: The Nose

As a writer, it would be hard to be more irrational than Nikolai Gogol (1809-51). His literary technique was whimsical, surreal, grotesque, Gothic, and absurd. Much of his work consists of satirical attacks on the tsarist bureaucracy, but there is also another Gogol, the man who was out to show that "reality" was unstable and untrustworthy. All of this took its toll, however. Gogol was a tormented soul, suffered from severe depression, and like Pushkin, died at a relatively young age.

Also like Pushkin, Gogol drew heavily on the Russian—in his case, Cossack and Ukrainian—folklore tradition. He was born and raised in the part of the Ukraine known as "Little Russia," a name particularly applied to the territory of a Cossack Hetmanate, a Ukrainian Cossack state.

His grandmother taught him old songs and scary folk tales, and he loved the customs and tales of that region. All of this found its way into his second book, *Evenings on a Farm near Dikanka* (1831-32), which was a roaring success. The characters are lurid, and include witches, buffoons, and devils. In "St. John's Eve," Petro, the protagonist, makes a pact with the devil: a treasure will be his if he sacrifices a child at a witches' sabbath. So he cuts off a little boy's head, monsters burst forth, and a witch laps up the blood. "A Terrible Vengeance," also part of this collection, "is littered with dreams, magic rituals, and corpses rising from their graves," according to his biographer, Henri Troyat. "Beneath the seemingly orderly face of nature," says Troyat, "writhe the forces of primal chaos."(1)

Gogol pretty much broke the mold. Troyat believes he sparked a renaissance in Russian literature, that he unleashed a force that nothing could stop. His quirky style had a major influence on Bulgakov, Dostoevsky, Franz Kafka, Yevgeny Zamyatin, Andrei Bely, Turgenev, Chekhov, Gorky, Tolstoy, and even Sholem Aleichem, despite the fact that Gogol was a rabid anti-Semite. The eminent Jewish author, who was a fellow Ukrainian, admired him greatly. Works such as "The Overcoat," "Diary of a Madman," *Dead Souls*, and *Taras Bulba* (a novel of Zaporog Cossack life, using folk legends as sources) are enduring classics, and it says something that more than 135 movies have been made based on these tales. Pushkin loved his work, and the two authors were close friends for several years. His short story "The Nose," written in 1834, first appeared in Pushkin's journal *Sovremennik* (The Contemporary) in 1836.(2)

Compared to the stories in *Evenings on a Farm*, "The Nose" is quite mild, although both combine the real and the supernatural. Many critics regard the story as an attack on the imperial bureaucracy—and a case can certainly be made for that argument—but I am going to leave that aspect aside in the following discussion, and concentrate on Gogol as master of the grotesque, and of sheer whimsy. I see the story as an exploration of surreal situations, and the notion that what we take to be reality is not carved in stone. It is also this aspect that is not only funny, but universal, transcending the boundaries of the Russian empire. When done well, the absurd and the surreal have enormous appeal.(3)

As with *The Queen of Spades,* our story takes place in St. Petersburg. The central character, who is a bit of a schmo, is a mid-level bureaucrat by the name of Platon Kovalyov (Ковалёв, in the original). One day he wakes up, looks at himself in the mirror, and sees that his nose is gone. Completely missing. Meanwhile, not too far away, on Voznesensky Avenue, a barber, one Ivan Yakovlevich, also wakes up, and sits down at the kitchen table, where his wife serves him a loaf of bread. Cutting the loaf in half, Ivan discovers that there is a nose inside of it.

But it gets even stranger, for Ivan, poor wretch, actually recognizes the nose. It belongs to one of his regular customers, Collegiate Assessor Kovalyov. "This is an impossible occurrence," Ivan tells himself; "after all, bread is something baked, and a nose is something altogether different." What to do? Ivan got dressed, wrapped the nose in a rag, and went out into the street. Walking, walking...when he arrived at St. Isaac's Bridge, over the Neva River, he bent over the railing and tossed the rag-with-nose into the water down below. As luck would have it, a policeman saw the whole thing, and presumably arrested him. "But here," writes Gogol, "the whole episode becomes shrouded in mist, and of what happened subsequently absolutely nothing is known."

But let us return to Kovalyov. Upon looking in the mirror and seeing a flat spot where his nose should have been, he immediately got dressed and went off to the chief of police. As there were no cabs around, he was forced to walk. Suddenly, he stopped in front of a house. A carriage drew up to the entrance, the doors opened, and a man in uniform—which was in fact Kovalyov's nose—jumped out, and ran up the stairs. Two minutes later, the Nose came out. He was elegantly dressed, in the outfit of a State Councillor. He got back into the carriage, which then drove off.

Kovalyov watched as the carriage then stopped at the Kazan Cathedral. The Nose went in, and Kovalyov followed him. When he approached the Nose, the latter was deep in prayer. Kovalyov wanted to engage him, but he didn't know what to say; and when he finally did, his words were incoherent. At last, he blurted out that the Nose was his own nose. The Nose told him that this was utter nonsense, got up, and left the cathedral.

Kovalyov pondered what to do next. He eventually found his way to the central newspaper office, intending to place an ad with a detailed description of the Nose. But the elderly clerk was not very helpful, inasmuch as he couldn't understand exactly what Kovalyov was trying to tell him. After a long silence, he told the latter that he couldn't place such an ad, as it would hurt the newspaper's reputation. To soften the rejection, he offered Kovalyov a pinch of snuff(!). Enraged by this total lack of sensitivity, Kovalyov ran out of the office in a huff, and went off to find the local police inspector, who also brushed him off. Thoroughly dejected, he returned home.

Shortly after, the same officer who witnessed Ivan Yakovlevich throwing a mysterious package into the Neva showed up at Kovalyov's door. "Did you happen to mislay your nose?" he asked him. Kovalyov answered in the affirmative. "Well," said the policeman, "he was intercepted on the point of leaving town. He was about to board a stagecoach and leave for Riga." With these words, he reached into his pocket and pulled out the Nose. Kovalyov was beside himself with joy.

When the police officer departed, Kovalyov went over to a mirror and tried to put the nose back in place. Horrors! It wouldn't stick. No matter how many times he tried, it simply refused to stay put. At this point of despair, Kovalyov had his servant summon his doctor. After a thorough examination, the doctor informed Kovalyov that he could indeed stick it on for him, but that the result would be worse than no nose at all. He advised Kovalyov to put the Nose in a jar of alcohol and sell it(!!).

Meanwhile, rumors began to spread regarding the Nose. For example, that it could be seen strolling along Nevsky Avenue every day at 3 p.m. The citizenry became excited; throngs gathered at the appointed hour, and chaos reigned supreme. The police were powerless against the crowds.

"Utterly nonsensical things happen in this world," Gogol concludes. For example, the Nose suddenly found itself back on Kovalyov's face, in the correct spot. So delighted was Kovalyov by this unexpected development that he wandered all over St. Petersburg, so that everyone could see that all was well in the nose department. Kovalyov was now always seen in good humor, smiling, and chasing the ladies.

So that is the end of our story, except for a short rumination by the author on how things that seem strange are not, perhaps, really all that strange. "After all," he asks the reader, "where aren't there incongruities?...Whatever anyone says, such things happen in this world; rarely, but they do."

As we might imagine, critics have had a field day with this tale; the supposed symbolism of the Nose has had numerous interpretations. And yet, there are a few observers, myself included, who just see Gogol as being whimsical, playful. I do believe, as stated earlier, that there is a theme here of reality not always being what it appears to be, and a number of Russian writers and artists, following in Gogol's footsteps, have taken up this theme in a more serious way. But for a man who was very depressed for much of his life, "The Nose" seems like a way of blowing (pardon the pun) off steam. Gogol was famous for his meticulous descriptions, for example, and in "The Nose" they are often hilarious. Here is his portrait of the doctor who visits Kovalyov, in the attempt to get the latter's nose back in place:

> The doctor was a fine figure of a man; he had beautiful pitch-black sidewhiskers, a fresh, healthy wife, ate raw apples first thing in the morning, and kept his mouth extraordinarily clean, rinsing it every morning for nearly three quarters of an hour and polishing his teeth with five different kinds of little brushes.

Can't you just see, in your mind's eye, this ridiculous, fastidious little man, whose best suggestion for Kovalyov's predicament is to put the Nose in a jar of alcohol and sell it? Gogol can be seen as something of a "trickster" figure, I suppose, and one literary critic regards the story as "a parable on the failure of all explanatory systems." After all, the whole incident is completely inexplicable.(4) It is no wonder that "The Nose," over time, penetrated the art, film, and literature of dozens of nations and cultures. Apparently, we could all use a good laugh, especially when it is at the expense of "reality."

Chapter 3

Lermontov: The Soul of a Cossack

Go to the Caucasus and you will return a poet.

—Mikhail Lermontov

Still just a boy, and he wrote *that!*

—Anton Chekhov, commenting on *A Hero of Our Time*

3. Mikhail Lermontov

Mikhail Lermontov (1814-41) is generally regarded as the writer who inherited the mantle of Pushkin, after the latter's death. In fact, his subsequent poem, "Death of the Poet," which more or less accused Russian high society of having had a role in that death, got him banished to the Caucasus in 1837, an exile that proved to be very creative for the writing he did there, including his great novel, *A Hero of Our Time*. "For a Russian writer," says Pushkin biographer T.J. Binyon, "the Caucasus, with its mountains and valleys, its fierce, independent, warring tribes, had the same exotic, romantic allure which the Levant had for Byron, or the American wilderness for Fenimore Cooper." *Hero* is a Romantic masterpiece, and was quickly recognized as such. It captured the spirit of the age, one characterized by a lack of meaning. Its anti-hero, Grigory Pechorin, is the archetypal alienated youth, or superfluous man, drifting along without any real purpose. His entire personality is one of detached (or affected) irony, a posture that the Russian youth of the time could easily identify with.(1)

My own connection to Lermontov is, oddly enough, rather personal.(2) When I was five years old, my maternal grandfather would occasionally babysit me when my parents were out for the evening, and I could hear him quietly singing to himself: *Vykhozhu odin ya na dorogu…*—"I set out on the road, alone." It's a mournful song, one of yearning. Many years later, I discovered that it was from a poem by Lermontov, written the year he died, 1841, and set to music twenty years later by Elizaveta Shashina. It sounds like Lermontov thinking back on his own life:

> From this life, there's nothing I require.
> From the past, there's nothing I regret...
> Let me lay forever in this orchard,
> In the shade of the rustling oak above.(3)

I also have a vague memory of my mother singing Lermontov's famous Cossack Lullaby to me, "Bayushki Bayu," another poem of great melancholy. Lermontov was in the Caucasus when he heard an old Terek Cossack woman singing this song, and transcribed it. The title is best translated as "Hushabye," and was sung to infants to get them to fall asleep. The mother sings:

> And you will have a Cossack's soul
> And be a champion high,
> When I come out to see you go,
> And you shall wave good-bye...
>
> And I shall think how, far away,
> You must be pining too;
> Oh, sleep, while not a care is yours,
> *Baioushki, baiou.*

One modern literary critic, Valentin Golovin, wrote that the Lullaby "went the whole round: from the original folklore source to literature, and from literature to living folklore."

Lermontov, according to biographer Laurence Kelly, endowed the Caucasus with qualities of mystery and purity—a lost paradise—and spent his life in search of these things. To have the soul of a Cossack was all he ever wanted.(4)

Lermontov's enchantment with the Caucasus occurred much earlier than his period of exile, however. Kelly tells us that he was taken there as a child, which was when he began to learn about this "wild, Eastern world": Tatars, Ossetians, Kabardins, Chechens, Ingushi, Avars, Lesghi. In the town of Pyatigorsk there was a storyteller named Shora Nogmov, who recited folk tales, which Lermontov eagerly absorbed. In fact, he later briefed Pushkin on the legends of these peoples.(5)

A good illustration of Lermontov's use of this material is his long narrative poem *The Song of the Merchant Kalashnikov* (1838). The story involves a love-triangle that takes place at the court of Ivan the Terrible (sixteenth century), in which a boxing match leads to the death of one of the rivals. The narrator, says biographer John Garrard, is "a stylized 'singer' in the old Russian folk tradition"; the tone and rhythm of the poem are that of the *byliny*, the old Russian oral epics. The poem, according to Garrard, shows that Lermontov was quite familiar with Russian folklore. As an exile, he studied the local languages of these "Eastern" peoples, and it inspired some of his work.(6)

In addition to his prolific literary output—thirty long poems, 600 minor ones, one novel, and five plays, all in the space of six years—he did some exquisite painting. In this, he was prolific as well, and Kelly reproduces a number of these—mostly landscapes of the Caucasus—in his biography. They are, in fact, stunning; Lermontov's deep feeling for the region comes through quite clearly.

4. Mikhail Lermontov, *View of Tiflis*, 1837

Lermontov died in Pyatigorsk, in a duel that, similar to the one that ended Pushkin's life, was frivolous, and could have been avoided. The funeral was held two days later; thousands turned out for it. To this day, and with some justification, Russians regard him as a national hero—a hero for all times, as it were. In terms of literary influence, Garrard contends that *A Hero of Our Times* was the first major novel in the Russian language, one that paved the way for the great psychological novels that followed—Tolstoy and Dostoevsky in particular. The influence on Chekhov was also significant. (7)

As for me, I can still hear my grandfather singing that song, seventy-five years later.

Chapter 4

Mussorgsky: Pictures at an Exhibition

[Mussorgsky] loves all that is coarse, crude, rough...But he has a real, even original, talent...[He] speaks a new language.

—Tchaikovsky, letter to Madame von Meck, 1878

5. Modest Mussorgsky

Mussorgsky: Pictures at an Exhibition

If you want to experience Dionysus in music, the works of Modest Mussorgsky (1839-81) would be a good place to start. So radical was his style, so powerful his compositions, that "amazing" seems almost lame as a description of his achievement. A raving alcoholic, largely self-taught, with no schooling in musical theory, it was almost as though he altered our understanding of sound, and of what it could do.(1)

There is no doubt that he was a musical prodigy. At age seven he was playing piano pieces by Liszt. At age twelve, he composed a polka. He went on to compose *Night on Bald Mountain* (1867); an opera based on a tale by Gogol (1868, unfinished); and a second opera based on Pushkin's *Boris Godunov* (1868-69). *Pictures at an Exhibition* followed in 1874; and along the way, sixty-five original songs.

Whence cometh all this energy? Mussorgsky was an ardent Slavophile, and his great ambition was to create a nationalistic school of Russian music. This meant delving into the peasant-folksong tradition, and his earliest exposure to this came from his grandmother/nanny Irina, who used to be a serf. When, in later years, he drew up an autobiographical sketch, he titled it "fairy tales and the spirit of folk-life." As one critic put it, his "musical style is irrevocably Russian and intently [sic] speaks of its peasants, folk tunes, and supernatural legends."(2) The opening section of *Night on Bald Mountain*, for example, literally reeks of witchery. All of this was part of Mussorgsky's opposition to Western music, and it showed up in his unorthodox use of tonality and harmony, as well as in his desire to have music tell a story in a "pictorial" or imagistic way. Clearly, we have left Mozart (and Apollo) far behind.(3)

Pictures at an Exhibition is one of his greatest compositions, and (happily for me) the first piece of classical music I ever listened to, at around age ten. My parents owned the vinyl LP of it, and I listened to it many times. Of course, at that age I hardly had any musical understanding of the work, but in the immortal words of Dwight Eisenhower, I knew what I liked. It represented itself in my mind as a series of stories, which created a pictorial narrative in my head. And so I imagined a dusty road in the Polish countryside, with cattle pulling a giant cart ("Bydło"), or a witch's hut in the woods standing on chicken legs ("Baba Yaga"), or "The Great Gate of Kiev." *Pictures*, writes Caryl Emerson, is "a work of great visual and rhythmic power...It is constructed so that we 'see' the content of the pictures." This, I believe I did see.

Mussorgsky's motivation for composing it was the death of his close friend Viktor Hartmann, an extremely talented architect and painter, in 1873, at the age of thirty-nine. Mussorgsky was devastated by this, but his grief was mollified somewhat by the decision of the Academy of Fine Arts in St. Petersburg to mount an exhibition of Hartmann's work, which took place in 1874. Mussorgsky attended the show and was deeply moved by it; the pictures rendered musically in *Pictures* are from that exhibition (most of them are now lost).

How to describe the break with Western music? As I understand it, Western polyphonic music (i.e., post-Gregorian chant) is characterized by harmonic lines or part-songs, and in general by a structure of tension and resolution. In its most basic form, you start with a melodic line, then go a few notes higher, then a few notes lower, and then return to the starting point (thereby resolving the tension). It's very predictable, and what Western audiences have come to expect. (For more on this see Chapter 8.) Mussorgsky's music, on the other hand, doesn't follow this classical symmetric pattern. The meter is *a*symmetrical; the music often lurches around unpredictably. In the piece called "Samuel Goldenberg and Schmuÿle" (a rich Jew and a poor one), Mussorgsky employs something similar to the Phrygian dominant scale, which is characteristic of Indian ragas and the music of the Near East; one also finds it in Hebrew prayers and in klezmer music. Part of "The Great Gate of Kiev" is based on a hymn of the Russian Orthodox Church (the chant of Znamenny). Hartmann was one of the first artists to include traditional Russian motifs and folklore in his work, and Mussorgsky picked up on this. Indeed, Orlando Figes writes that *Pictures* "created a new Russian language in music." Shifting tones and uneven rhythms are the distinctive features of peasant chant, and this went on to characterize Russian music from Mussorgsky to Stravinsky. Shostakovich and Prokofiev are part of this legacy.

Figes goes on to characterize Mussorgsky as a "Holy Fool." He was interested in the content of music, not its formal laws, and *Pictures* reflects a direct approach to life. "At its heart," says Figes, "is the magic reach and power of the Russian folk imagination." The closing piece, "The Great Gate of Kiev," is rooted in the sounds of Byzantium, and concludes with the glorious ringing of heavy church bells—"a picture of all of Russia drawn in sound."

Of course, all of this is like describing sex, as opposed to having it. I can only urge the reader to obtain the CD and listen to this last cut. Just let it wash over you; "glorious" is indeed the best way to describe it. It affects me as much at age eighty, as it did at ten.

Chapter 5

Chekhov: The Siren

It is [Chekhov's] works which I would take on a trip to another planet.

—Vladimir Nabokov

6. Anton Chekhov

Chekhov: The Siren

Without a doubt, Anton Chekhov (1860-1904) remains one of the greatest fiction writers of all time. Russian, yet universal. His four great plays—*The Seagull, Uncle Vanya, Three Sisters*, and *The Cherry Orchard*—are still performed to this day. He was a very serious and dedicated individual, yet many of his short stories, such as "The Siren" (1887), are extremely funny. He had a sense of humor that was both sly and dry. Chekhov was also a doctor, and a humanitarian, typically treating his patients for free. Russians adore him, and with good reason.

If there was a central drama in his life, it was the tension between science and religion; another formulation, perhaps, of the Dionysus-Apollo dialectic. Chekhov had a religious upbringing, but later education—he trained as a physician, after all—led him to declare himself an atheist. And yet, that old pull of magic and mystery stayed with him, and shows up in quite a few of his stories. Thus one of his biographers, Donald Rayfield, writes that "Chekhov's prose is imbued with intense love of the archaic language of the liturgy." His story "The Night Before Easter," for example, is clearly a mystical tale. The central character, Ieronim (Jerome), is a ferryman who takes people across a river to a monastery, where Easter is being celebrated. Chekhov shifts back and forth between the real and the surreal, or the ethereal. One critic notes that "the riverbank and monastery come alive as though part of an enchanted landscape." The narrator of the story describes the surroundings as "a magician's land," and indeed, Chekhov's ability to evoke an atmosphere is unequalled. The tale ends on a note of ambiguity. Ieronim represents someone or something—a man? a myth?—but Chekhov leaves it up to the reader to decide.(1)

Rayfield describes the two aspects of Chekhov as one being "the analytical follower of Turgenev and Tolstoy, the other [that of a] visionary prose-poet."(2) But the two aspects worked together, as it were. Chekhov never seemed to be tortured by the dialectic of rational/nonrational, as was the case with many other Russian writers. As an adult, he lived in the rational world, but in some of his writings, the nonrational world poked its nose through the rational curtain. This balancing act was, I'm guessing, a major source of his creativity. We can understand Nabokov's praise of the man (epigraph above): Chekhov is quite simply a pleasure to read.

"The Night Before Easter" is a very serious story, and a rather mysterious one; but Chekhov could also be light and witty in dealing with the nonrational, and this renders a story like "The Siren" downright hilarious. Apollo struggles with Dionysus, but by the end of the tale, it's a rout: Dionysus wins hands down.(3)

A few words about sirens are in order before we turn to Chekhov's treatment of their seductive voice. The classic story, of course, is in Book XII of the *Odyssey*, where Odysseus, on the advice of the sorceress Circe, had the crew of his ship plug their ears with wax, so that they would not be driven mad by the siren's enchanting song. (The ship was going home, in the aftermath of the Trojan War.) He himself wanted to hear the song, but in order not to be lured into madness by it, had himself tied to the mast, with strict orders to the crew not to let him go. The idea here is that the voice of

Chekhov: The Siren

the siren is so seductive, so powerful, that those who hear it are overwhelmed by desire, so much so that it can lead them to insanity, even death. Dionysus to the max, in other words.

Chekhov was fully aware of this passage in the *Odyssey*, and adapted it to a Russian context, in which the call of the wild was—food. One might even call his version a type of "gastronomic pornography." Nevertheless, he begins on a sober Apollonian note. The scene is a court room. The trial is apparently over, and a group of magistrates sit around, waiting for their chairman—Chekhov calls him the "Presiding Judge"—to write his dissenting opinion (he didn't agree with the verdict). They are all hungry, looking forward to going home and having dinner. The court secretary, a man named Zhilin, begins to talk about a dinner he once had, and about the pleasures of eating in general. He speaks in a low voice, almost a whisper. Slowly, his speech gains momentum, becoming increasingly passionate. Real appetite, he says, is of "the wolfish sort, when you're ready to make a meal of your own father." "Once when I was travelling," he goes on, "I closed my eyes and imagined sucking-pig with horse-radish, and got such an appetite that it made me quite hysterical." "An expression of beatitude" spread across his face.

> What about appetizers? The best, he tells the group, is herring: You eat a bit of herring with onion and mustard sauce, and without waiting, my friend, while the sparks are still flying in the stomach, you help yourself to caviar, with lemon juice, if you prefer it that way, then you have a radish with salt, and another piece of herring. But I'll tell you what's better still, my

friend: salted pink mushrooms, minced, as fine as caviar and served with onion and olive oil….

And then there is the meat pie. Chekhov's description amounts to pure sex:

> The meat pie must make your mouth water, it must lie there before you, naked, shameless, a temptation! You wink at it, you cut off a sizable slice, and you let your fingers just play over it, this way, out of excess of feeling. You eat, the butter drips from it like tears, and the filling is fat, juicy, rich, with eggs, giblets, onions…

Turning to borscht, Zhilin says that it should be "prepared with sugar beets, Ukrainian style, you know the way, my friend, with ham and country sausages. It should be served with sour cream, of course, and a sprinkling of fresh parsley and dill." By the time he gets around to describing roast duck with potatoes, "browned to a turn and soaked with duck fat," his colleagues start to grab their hats and run out of the room. Not to be fazed, he continues: "After the roast, sir, a man is full, and he goes off into a sweet eclipse. The body is basking, the soul is transported." Add a glass of brandy, and "your whole being is suffused with a kind of fragrance." By now it's a stampede, as the room empties out. The dissenting opinion is left behind, in the dust, as the Presiding Judge himself finally flees the chamber.

Zhilin, of course, is a siren. He urges his colleagues to avoid anything intellectual, and to indulge their sensual desires instead. Chekhov, says one literary critic, opens us up to "the sensuality of the world." In his work, memory and imagination are closely linked to the body, the power of which is overwhelming. In fact, desire finally turns into hysteria; the voice of the siren drives the intellectual Apollonian magistrates completely bonkers. Imagine their agony, if they had been tied to a mast, without benefit of wax.(4)

Personally, I find Chekhov's ability to combine wit and intensity absolutely remarkable. As I read the story I was laughing...and also found myself getting hungry. Like Walt Whitman, Chekhov was large; he contained multitudes. He took in the entire world, dross and all, and turned it into gold. As he faced death, the light touch was still with him. His last words were, "I haven't had champagne for a long time." I doubt I'll be that cavalier when my time is up.

Chapter 6

Bely

The world is not logical; it is *psycho*-logical.

—Goethe

7. Andrei Bely

One would think that with Gogol, surrealism, and the Apollo-Dionysus dialectic, had reached their apogee in Russian literature. It turns out that Boris Nikolaevich Bugaev, popularly known as Andrei Bely (1880-1934), not only pushed the envelope, but left it far behind. Vladimir Nabokov regarded Bely's novel *Petersburg* (serialized during 1913-14) as one of the four great novels of the twentieth century, the other three being *Ulysses* (Joyce), *In Search of Lost Time* (Proust), and *Metamorphosis* (Kafka). What adjectives, aside from surreal, can describe it? Dazzling? Kaleidoscopic? Delirious? Cryptic? Take your pick. Reviewing it in the *New York Times*, Simon Karlinsky, at the time distinguished scholar of Russian literature at UC Berkeley, called it "the most important, most influential and most perfectly realized Russian novel written in the 20th century," adding that Bely "is the man who affected the development of modern Russian prose more than any other 20th-century figure." In terms of this genre, I doubt that Bely was ever surpassed.(1)

Let's back up a moment. *Petersburg* was preceded by *The Silver Dove* (1909), which is set (like *Petersburg*) during the abortive revolution of 1905. The protagonist is Pyotr Daryalsky, whose name derives from a gorge in the Caucasus. For reasons he himself does not understand, he leaves his lovely girlfriend Katya and gets involved with a rough peasant woman named Matryona, who "converts him to [an] eschatological and Dionysian sect of religious dissenters." He aspires to a spiritual union with "the people"; the adventure turns out to be a complete disaster. Similar themes show up in *Petersburg*, and, says Karlinsky, evoke the flavor of Gogol.(2)

The book reminds me of a line from Wittgenstein, to the effect that an increase in the precision or logic of communication often leads, paradoxically, to a decrease in meaning, or understanding. I have elsewhere described this as the difference between intellectual and ontological knowing. The latter, derived from the Greek word *ontos* (being), is visceral, or intuitive. Perhaps this is a variant on the Apollo-Dionysus distinction. In the novel, Apollonian thought is identified w/authority, Dionysian thought with revolution. The conflict plays out in an Oedipal way, although it would seem that by the end, Bely has managed to merge the two. In any case, it bears out Wittgenstein's claim, in that (to me, at least) the book captures the essence of the 1905 revolution, and its deep cross-currents, far better than any scholarly study. Thus John Elsworth, Bely's translator, wrote that "Time does not move in straight lines here, it turns back to devour its own tail, and it is only in myth that anything can be truly explained."(3)

In any case, Bely was no slouch when it came to an understanding of social and historical process, but he filtered the latter through the lens of mysticism, in particular the work of the Austrian occultist Rudolf Steiner, with whom he was friends. Karlinsky notes that his language is all over the place: scientific, colloquial, psychoanalytic, peasant-based, and filled with puns and invented words. A formula for incomprehension, one would think, and yet Wittgenstein's assertion rings true: Bely's message is quite comprehensible. In a word, he was (like Wittgenstein) an ontological genius.

A perfect example of ontological analysis: the central theme, says Karlinsky, is that of a love-hate relationship between a high-ranking cabinet member and his son, who is involved in the revolutionary movement. In effect, the 1905 revolution in microcosm (or a crucial aspect of it). Karlinsky goes on: "Bely's devastating demonstration of the erotic and sado-masochistic nature of the impulses that underlie both reactionary repression and revolutionary terror—and of the ease with which the one can become the other," is a profound revelation for the twentieth century. Revelation, or uncanny prediction? How much of that switching have we seen, during the previous 100+ years? How many millions of lives were lost —and continue to be lost—due to ontological blindness? Cultural analyst Michael Buening puts it this way:

> *Petersburg* is about one event as a perpetual moment in history, a constancy of new orders usurping old orders and children destroying and then becoming parents… [I]t is eerily prescient in predicting how the initial euphoria, the bomb explosion of Communism, would scorch the earth as badly as any tsar did.(4)

—Revolution as a revolving door, in short.

I'm going to return to Bely's style, use of language, surreal sequences and so on, in a moment. Before we go any further with that, however, let's take a look at the plot.

Nikolai Apollonovich Ableukhov, a philosophy student who is part of a radical political group, and who can also be characterized as a loser and a ne'er-do-well (a putz, in Yiddish), is given a time bomb and a task: to murder a senior government official, who just so happens to be his father, Apollon Apollonovich Ableukhov. (I'm guessing that the repeated use of "Apollo" is quite intentional on Bely's part.) The bomb is given to him by a fellow radical, Alexander Ivanovich Dudkin, whose "boss" is Nikolai Stepanovich Lippanchenko (also known as Lipensky). If this forest of names were not enough, the bomb itself, which is stashed in a sardine can(!), has a (ridiculous) name: Pepp Peppovich Pepp. After a series of bizarre and meaningless adventures, Nikolai finally manages to plant the bomb in his father's bedroom. It goes off, but Apollon is not killed. End of story.

Searching the Internet for a narration of the plot, one discovers that very little has been written about it. It's an Oedipal drama, and it fails, period. The plot, such as it is, resembles a stew, through which the reader has to swim. What we find is Steiner, Theosophy, Eastern religion, psychoanalysis, and various dream-like sequences. *Petersburg* is suffused by strange mental states, with Nikolai running around in a red "domino" suit, going to parties, and pursuing a woman who has no interest in him. As such, he comes off (correctly) as a fool, and is the subject of various gossip columns in the newspapers. If I had to capture the story in a single phrase, I would call it "a confused soul-journey."

Hence, critics of the text are not exercised by plot. What they want to talk about, among other things, are the influences on Bely (e.g., Nietzsche and Dostoevsky) and/or the writers he influenced (e.g., Zamiatin and Babel). A host of interpretations abound, Freud being one of the most convincing. Some commentators see the story as the forthright war between Apollo and Dionysus, with which I obviously agree. And the political dimension reflects the individual, psychological one, in that the object of the 1905 revolution was to overthrow the tsar (archetypal father). Hovering over all of this is a pervasive sense of doom, of imminent disaster. In many ways, it's a gloomy book.

Here is an excerpt from the text that conveys the flavor of Bely's style; it all takes place in a dream (or dream-state) of the protagonist:

> The Day of Judgement was at hand...
>
> [H]e planned to throw a bomb at his father; to throw a bomb at swift-flowing time itself. But his father was Saturn, the cycle of time turned upon itself, and closed; the empire of Saturn returned...
>
> Bereft of body; still he felt his body: some invisible centre that had previously been both his consciousness and his "self," turned out to possess a semblance of the former, burnt to ashes: Nikolai Apollonovich's logical premises turned into bones; the syllogisms around these bones wrapped themselves into rigid sinews; the content of his logical activity developed flesh and skin; and so the "self" of Nikolai Apollonovich again displayed its bodily form, although it was not a body; and in this *non-body* (in the exploded "self") someone else's "self" was revealed: this "self" had rushed in from Saturn and to Saturn it returned.(5)

Saturn, here, refers to the classic myth, in which the old man devours his children, who later return to kill him—the revolution eating itself. It is the subject of one of Goya's most famous, and most disturbing, paintings: *Saturno devorando a su hijo*. Again, the point of the novel is pretty clear.

To all of this, Bely added an Epilogue. It is years later; Apollon Apollonovich is long-gone; Nikolai has left Russia, and is now living in a little house he rented from an Arab in a village in Tunisia.

> The sun's flame is ferocious: it fills the eyes with purple; if you turn round—it strikes furiously at the nape of your neck; it makes the desert look greenish and deathly; however, life itself is deathly; it would be good to stay here forever…

As for Bely's legacy: unlike *The Master and Margarita* (see Chapter 9), *Petersburg* is far too cryptic to have become popular, or to have had much of an impact, except in esoteric circles, such as the Russian Symbolist movement or the Modernist school (themselves fairly esoteric). He rarely appears on the syllabi of university literature courses, for example. Bely fell out of favor after the Revolution of 1917, and died in relative poverty. And yet, for those of us lucky enough to have stumbled across his work, the reaction tends to be one of awe: "My God, that a human being could have actually brought something like this into the world!"

Chapter 7

Diaghilev & Co.: Les Ballets Russes

[T]he passage of time will...show the true significance of this elemental being, one of the most curious and characteristic figures of our country, who brought together in his person all the fabulous beauty and all the inexhaustible might of Russian culture.

—Alexander Benois, letter to Walter Nouvel, a few days after Diaghilev's death in 1929

...that ogre, that sacred monster...that Russian prince to whom life was tolerable only to the extent to which he could summon up marvels.

—Jean Cocteau, 1912

8. Sergei Diaghilev

He lived and died "a favorite of the gods." For he was a pagan, and a Dionysian pagan—not an Apollonian. He loved everything earthly—earthly love, earthly passions, earthly beauty...That doesn't mean he had no religious feeling. But that feeling was pagan rather than Christian. Instead of faith he had superstition, instead of the fear of God terror of the universe and its secrets, instead of Christian meekness a delicate, almost childlike tenderness.

—Igor Stravinsky, letter to Walter Nouvel, a week after Diaghilev's death

Stravinsky (and Cocteau) got it mostly right: Sergei (or Serge) Diaghilev (1872-1929), the great impresario of ballet, opera, and dance, was certainly a Dionysian figure, but not without an Apollonian side. A blend of the two, if you will, with the scales tipped heavily toward the Dionysian. But he had powerful rational, i.e., organizational, skills. He knew how to arrange things for maximum effect, how to negotiate and navigate the social and economic world, how to edit a musical score, and so on. (This even extended to drawing up contracts with security personnel and coat-check girls.) During the course of his adult life, Diaghilev was able to pull off very difficult projects, to make things happen in the real world. As he wrote to his stepmother in 1895,

> [F]irst of all I am a great charlatan, although one with flair; second I'm a great charmer; third I've great nerve; fourth I'm a man with a great deal of logic and few principles; and fifth, I think I lack talent; but if you

like, I think I've found my real calling—patronage of the arts.

As one of his biographers put it, he understood "that his genius lay not in artistic creation, but in perceiving the genius of others."(1)

These Apollonian talents also showed up in Diaghilev's theoretical analysis of the arts. In 1898 he launched the very influential journal, *Mir iskusstva*—The World of Art—in which he stated that its purpose was to serve "the god of Apollo," i.e., modern art. In the first few issues, he published a long article setting out his theoretical position on the arts ("Difficult Questions"). He also drew leading artistic and intellectual talents into its orbit, including Léon Bakst and Andrei Bely.(2)

But all of this was ultimately in the service of Dionysian excitement, drama, immense creativity, and the breaking of the boundaries of cultural norms. Diaghilev was a force to be reckoned with, and it probably is no exaggeration to say that he turned the art world upside down. He drew on pagan sources, on the folkloric tradition of peasant Russia, for much of his inspiration. The result was an enduring success. As one art critic put it, "His greatest achievement was to ensure the close integration of story, music, choreography and design, creating spectacles where the overall impact surpassed the parts." In so doing, remarked Coco Chanel, who was a costume designer (and financial supporter) of the Ballets Russes, "Diaghilev invented Russia for foreigners." The B.R., wrote Janet Flanner in the *New Yorker*, "left its racial imprint on every land it visited." It contained a "cargo of exotic, thick-thighed dancers, Slavic sceneries, strange music, heretical ideas, and graceful, sensuous satisfactions."(3)

In addition, Diaghilev managed to turn his exhibitions into great social events. Especially noteworthy is the crowd of composers he drew on during the early years: Debussy, Ravel, Satie, Manuel de Falla, Richard Strauss, Sergei Prokofiev, Ottorino Respighi, and Francis Poulenc. A similar constellation of stars was often seen at dress rehearsals: Cocteau, Gide, Bonnard, Vuillard, Hugo von Hofmannsthal, and so on.

The theme running through so many of the impresario's productions was the ecstatic, nonrational dimension of life, Slavic and oriental exoticism in particular, which catapulted the Ballets Russes (founded in 1909) to instant fame, and nearly twenty-five years of leadership of the dance world. "What the Parisians especially liked," writes music critic Ivan Hewett, "was the way these 'Northern Savages' (as one critic called the company) played to the fashion for everything primitive and untamed." As historian Modris Ecksteins put it,

> It was in the Russian countryside, primitive and unaffected by mechanism, that Diaghilev and his circle found much of their inspiration, in the designs and colors of peasant costumes, the paintings of carts and sleighs, the carvings around windows and doors, and the myths and fables of an unassuming rural culture.(4)

Given that the artistic output of Diaghilev and the Ballets Russes was so massive, I'm going to restrict this discussion to some of the highlights of 1905-15, just to convey an idea of what the man was capable of.

-Diaghilev organized two major art exhibitions in Paris during 1905-6. The one in 1905 had more than 4,000 paintings; Diaghilev himself traveled around to acquire these items from 450 owners. In the space of three months, 45,000 people attended it. The one in 1906, designed by Bakst, was a bit more modest, with 750 works. Like the previous exhibition, it was a huge success. (See below on Bakst.)(5)

-In 1908, he mounted a production of Mussorgsky's opera, *Boris Godunov*, at the Paris Opéra house. For this, Diaghilev sent Ivan Bilibin to villages in the North, to buy old traditional dresses, embroidered fabric, and head coverings. (Bilibin was a famous illustrator whose work was inspired by Russian folk tales and Slavic folklore. He later designed sets and costumes for the Ballets Russes.) Feodor Chaliapin was in the starring role. The reception was terrific.(6)

-The premiere of the Ballets Russes took place in Paris on 19 May 1909, and featured three pieces: *Pavillon d'Armide, Prince Igor*, and *Le Festin*. It went down as a legendary event, partly due to the participation of Vaslav Nijinsky. Contemporary sources called it life-changing; the critics raved. One wrote that Nijinsky's "elevation is such that he appears to fly through the air like a bird." Also in 1909 was *Cléopâtre*, which launched Bakst's career as a creator of exotic sets and costumes that evoked the mystery of the East.(7)

-1910 saw the production of *The Firebird*, again at the Paris Opéra, with music by Stravinsky, who became famous overnight as a result. The firebird is an old, legendary figure in Russian folk tales, and the libretto drew on the anthology of Alexander Afanasyev, the great nineteenth-century Slavic folklorist and ethnographer. Costume designs were by Bakst and Alexander Golovin, which included a dress largely made of feathers for the lead dancer, Tamara Karsavina. When she danced, the feathers created a magical flying effect. *Firebird* was followed by *Scheherazade*, which created a great stir, inasmuch as it depicted violence and Eastern sensuality, along with primitivist themes. Bakst's sets for this were spectacular, employing vibrant colors and costly materials.(8)

-Stravinsky drew on folk music, and legends, for *Petrushka*, 1911. This is the story of three puppets brought to life by a charlatan figure, or magician. Petrushka is the main character of Russian folk puppet shows that go back to the seventeenth century. The three puppets live out a tale of love and jealousy. Petrushka is often seen as a trickster figure, one who injects chaos into rational order.(9)

-A new ballet for 1912 was called *Thamar*, which was an exotic Caucasian tale. But much more significant was *L'après-midi d'un faune*. It's a short piece by Debussy, and was choreographed by Nijinsky, under Diaghilev's guidance. Nijinsky wore a fig-leaf body stocking designed by Bakst, and there is a scene in which he simulates masturbation. The audience had a hard time with it; the editor of *Figaro* called it "filthy and bestial." Auguste Rodin, however, defended it in the press.(10)

-The debut of *The Rite of Spring* on 29 May 1913 is a legendary event in the history of ballet, and a milestone in the history of music. The music was by Stravinsky, which broke with traditional Western rhythms (see Chapter 8); the choreography and dance were by Nijinsky. The story, which is effectively a celebration of Dionysian energy, is based on pagan myths: we see various primitive rituals celebrating the coming of spring, then a young girl is chosen as a sacrificial victim, and dances herself to death, in what one drama critic referred to as a "strange dance of religious hysteria." The evening before, the entire company, including Diaghilev, Nijinsky, Stravinsky, André Gide, Bakst, and Maurice Ravel predicted it would cause a scandal, and they were right. According to some witnesses, a riot broke out, and canes were brandished all over the theater, in threat of combat. The German diplomat Harry Kessler wrote in his diary, "A new type of savagery in art and anti-art at once: all form is destroyed, and a new form suddenly emerges from the chaos." Years later the London *Times* wrote that *The Rite of Spring* was to the twentieth century what Beethoven's Ninth was to the nineteenth. It is noteworthy that over 200 different versions of the ballet have been choreographed since that first performance.(11)

-As for the 1914 season, the hit this time around was *Le Coq d'Or*. The designer was Natalia Goncharova, who came up with brilliant designs inspired by Russian folk art and Slavic exoticism. For example, she drew on the popular prints known as *lubki*. Like Diaghilev, her goal was to use ideas from the past to create something new in the present. Guillaume Apollinaire wrote a rave review of the show, the opening of which was attended by Max Jacob, Blaise Cendrars, Coco Chanel, Brancusi, Robert Delaunay, Braque, Picasso, André Derain, Marcel Duchamp, Juan Gris, Fernand Léger, and Modigliani.(12)

-Plans for 1915 included a ballet based on ancient Russian peasant wedding rituals, and another one set in the prehistoric world of the Scythians.(13)

-Looking ahead, Picasso was part of the company by 1917, and in the 1920s Diaghilev picked Matisse, Braque, and other famous French artists to design various productions.(14)

And this (above) was only ten years of the man's life, which should give us some idea of what he managed to accomplish in the long run. He did indeed, as Jean Cocteau put it, summon up marvels. His Dutch biographer, Sjeng Scheijan, wrote that Diaghilev "squeezed every last drop out of life, living in the eye of a whirlwind of joy and sorrow, conflict and reconciliation, a personal cloud of turbulence that left those around him breathless." In fact, his legacy was enormous; he effectively changed the face of modern dance. And many of the Ballets Russes members went on to found major dance schools, e.g., George Balanchine in America, or Tamara Karsavina in England. Ballet scores by Stravinsky and others continue to be performed to this day, and the repertoire of the company remains a treasure trove for modern choreographers. *Res ipsa loquitur*; the record speaks for itself.(15)

Personally, I find it hard to write about Diaghilev, because ultimately he had very little in the way of actual content. Rather, he was a facilitator for the content of others, a cultural entrepreneur, as it were. As a result, he was a genius in a category he himself had invented. Diaghilev was *sui generis*; I can't think of anyone like him. The real story of Diaghilev is a series of figures he put on the map, such as Nijinsky, for example, or Anna Pavlova. "Diaghilev's Empire," as biographer Rupert Christiansen puts it, consisted of a galaxy of talent. At this point, we could discuss Nijinsky, Bakst, Stravinsky, Goncharova, and a host of others, all of whom were part of that galaxy. The problem, however, is that to really give a full accounting of, say, Nijinsky, we would have to see him dance (but see Film Nijinsky 1912 - YouTube); for Bakst, to view his sumptuous costumes and set designs (easily accessible on the Internet, e.g., V&A · Léon Bakst – Design For The Ballet (vam.ac.uk)); for Stravinsky, his music (e.g., Igor Stravinsky - The Rite of Spring (1913) - YouTube); and so on. In what follows I am going to discuss the huge contribution of Bakst. As for Stravinsky, he deserves a chapter of his own.(16)

Of course, he wasn't born Léon Bakst; that came later. Originally, he was Lev Samoylovich Rosenberg, from Grodno Gobernaya (White Russia), and he lived from 1866 to 1924, dying near Paris, where he spent most of his adult life. As we saw above, he designed Diaghilev's 1906 art exhibition, and was in on the ground floor of *Mir iskusstva* and the Ballets Russes. He did the logo and graphics for the former, which brought him some degree of fame (including a commission for some artwork for Tsar Nicholas II in 1902). From 1908, he did the scenery for a whole string of Ballets Russes productions, including *Cleopatra, Scheherazade, Firebird,* and *L'après-midi d'un faune*. In effect, he became the B.R.'s unofficial set designer and artistic director.

Bakst's set and dress designs were extraordinary. Violent, extravagant, opulent, Oriental, lush, sensual, erotic, exotic—these are the adjectives that best describe his work, and led to his international fame. Energy burst forth from every pore, as it were, and the French were intoxicated. As noted above, *Scheherazade* was over the top. In the wake of it, Diaghilev proclaimed him "the hero of our ballet," and members of the cast put him on their shoulders and carried him around the stage. Bonnard, Seurat, and other notables of the artworld applauded him. He was interviewed everywhere; he cofounded a successful textile business; his paintings were installed in prestigious galleries; and his impact on fashion was huge, as women started wearing Bakstian costumes, which included Tatar and Cossack outfits and Russian peasant clothing. Cole Porter referred to him in one of his songs, and his student Marc Chagall described how inspiring Bakst was for him. Plus, he wrote books and articles on the history and theory of art. Could his star rise any higher? It did, for several years.

Interestingly enough, like Diaghilev, Bakst also possessed a strong Apollonian streak. In 1909 he published an essay in a journal called *Apollon*, entitled "The Paths of Classicism in Art," in which he predicted that the art of the future would be "deliberately uncomplicated," moving towards "a new and very simple form." What was in store for us, he told his readers, was "a new classical art." Bakst was not only brilliant; he was also very complex.(17)

Bakst ended his relationship with Diaghilev and the Ballets Russes in 1918, and from that point on his star began to slowly wane (although he continued to paint). Not much is heard of him, or written about him, one hundred years later. But for a long time he was indeed, as Diaghilev said, a hero—and not just for the B.R. His raw Dionysian energy captivated all of Apollonian Europe, and the fact is that very few artists have been able to duplicate his achievement in the fields of costume and design. When Bakst died, in 1924, the funeral procession included some of the most famous artists of the day. His subsequent obscurity is surely our loss.

As for Stravinsky, his star never waned. Many historians and musicians regard him as the greatest composer of the twentieth century. Which is probably true, but he was also very talented at self-promotion, at fashioning an image. His dominance over the century's music, in other words, was not an accident. As one of his biographers put it, he was not only Stravinsky; he was also "Stravinsky." And like Bakst, he was a bundle of contradictions, but in his case they enabled him to endure.(18)

Chapter 8

Stravinsky: The Rite of Spring

[Stravinsky] has opened yet another door, and there everything is permitted, everything is sonorous, joyous, and each note takes you by surprise, just as you would wish—and overwhelms you.

—Misia Sert, letter to Jean Cocteau, 1915

[Stravinsky is] the musician par excellence of modern life…Ingenious and trivial, knowing and sceptical, half human and half mechanised—is not modern life all that, like Stravinsky's music?

—Richard Capell in the *Daily Telegraph* (London), 1934

9. Igor Stravinsky

Stravinsky: The Rite of Spring

Don't you get it? This piece is all about SEX!

—Leonard Bernstein, at a rehearsal of *The Rite of Spring* at the Schleswig-Holstein Musik Festival in Germany, 1988

"Our greatest musician," pianist Misia Sert called him, in her 1915 letter to Cocteau. Trying to write a sketch of Stravinsky is more than daunting; his was a towering talent, *sans pareil*, and the literature on him is correspondingly enormous. His particular gift was his ability to fuse the modern with the peasant-shamanic tradition of Old Russia, a dynamic with which he had to struggle, however. This dialectic of Apollo vs. Dionysus defined his creative-professional life. It was also precisely what his Parisian audiences wanted to hear—a dynamic that meshed perfectly with the times: the primitive reconfigured as modern.

Igor Stravinsky grew up in a small town west of St. Petersburg, Oranienbaum (later renamed Lomonosov). He lived from 1882 to 1971. He was a French citizen from 1934, and an American one as of 1945. He lived in Paris during 1920-39, and moved to Beverly Hills in 1940, where he became friends with Aldous Huxley, who lived nearby. Then to West Hollywood in 1941. Other visitors included Christopher Isherwood and Dylan Thomas. In 1947 he began a collaboration with W.H. Auden that proved to be very successful. At the time of his death he was living on Fifth Avenue in Manhattan, having moved to New York in 1969.(1)

Stravinsky had a rather sharp ambivalence toward his Russian roots. The whole folkloric tradition was central to his work, especially in the early years. Later, he tried to cover it up somewhat, and reinvent himself as a cultured and cosmopolitan West European. This tension never really went away. In his autobiography (ghost-written by his friend and assistant, Walter Nouvel), Stravinsky talks about his memory of the music of the peasantry, to which he had been exposed during vacations his family took in the countryside—specifically, the unison singing of the women on their way home from work. He was able to imitate these songs as late as the 1950s.(2)

The truth is that Stravinsky was deeply engaged with Russian folklore. At one point, he sent Diaghilev Afanasyev's collection of folktales (referred to in Chapter 7), for him to search for new themes. Many of the melodies in *The Rite of Spring* come from folk tunes, and the opening bassoon solo is actually an old Lithuanian wedding song. Rural life, including peasant costumes and music, got incorporated into the ballet *Petrushka*. This was also true of *The Firebird* and the ballet *Les Noces* (The Wedding), the latter of which used a 3/4 and 4/4 time structure, very different from the norm of Western music. Writing in the *New Yorker* (in 1935), Janet Flanner said that this ballet was developed "from the rhythmically interesting hiccups of two drunken peasants" whom Stravinsky happened to sit next to, at one point.(3)

Stravinsky began taking lessons in composition from Rimsky-Korsakov in 1905. The two of them worked on a symphony, incorporating Russian folk tunes. Another early piece was the *Scherzo fantastique*, which was conducted in 1909. As it turned out, Diaghilev was in the audience, and remarked to his manager that the piece had "a tonal quality that should surprise the public." He sent Stravinsky his card, asking him to call on him. This meeting effectively launched the young composer's career, and was the beginning of a long-term collaboration. Both men proved to be very successful in "surprising the public."(4)

And so *The Firebird* premiered on 25 June 1910 at the Paris Opéra. It was constructed from a variety of fairy tales, mostly from the collection by Afanasyev. The story is one of a magical kingdom and creatures. Musically, it had many striking effects, such as a glissando of string harmonics at the beginning. (Glissando: a continuous slide upward or downward between two notes) The harmonies were exotic, especially the use of an eight-note diminished (octatonic) scale. (A symmetric scale composed of alternating whole and half steps) But, says biographer Jonathan Cross, "what *The Firebird* demonstrated beyond doubt was Stravinsky's instinct for the role music could play in the theatre…In transferring the techniques of opera to ballet the contribution of Stravinsky to the reinvention of dance for the twentieth century cannot be underestimated."(5)

The success of the ballet became an entrée into the wealthiest and most influential circles in Paris. Diaghilev hailed him as "the boy genius of Russian music." "He is a man on the eve of celebrity," the maestro declared. He wanted to spotlight him, create a buzz around him, and in fact, the audience went wild. Stravinsky was called back to the stage several times. He did, per Diaghilev, become an overnight sensation. His life, and the life of music itself, were changed forever. A few months after the premiere, Debussy wrote to a colleague that Stravinsky "has an instinctive genius for colour and rhythm…

[his music] is at once child-like and savage." And shortly after that, when he obtained a copy of the score for *Petrushka*, Debussy wrote directly to the man himself: "It is full of a kind of sonic magic, a mysterious transformation of the mechanical souls that become human through a magic spell...You will produce greater works than *Petrushka*, but this is already a feather in your cap."(6)

Petrushka was premiered by the Ballets Russes in 1911. Petrushka is a stock character of Russian folk puppetry. As noted in Chapter 7, he and two other puppets are brought to life by a magician, and live out a sad tale of love and jealousy. Despite its folk origins (it makes use of a number of folk tunes), the ballet marks the beginning of Stravinsky as a modernist, employing cascades of arpeggios (a type of broken chord whose notes are played in a rising or descending order). Jonathan Cross elaborates on the technique:

> Borrowed musical materials are fractured, reconfigured, denied their expected development. Stravinsky seems to be longing to return to a world that he knows has already been shattered...In this sense the musical fragmentation speaks presciently of the rapidly changing world in which he lived. The resulting sense of alienation is embodied in the character of the suffering Petrushka, whose part-human, part-puppet sides cannot be reconciled.(7)

Which brings us to *The Rite of Spring*, briefly discussed in the previous chapter. This particular ballet, partly due to the riot that broke out at its premiere, became very famous, and deserves an extended discussion. (At this point the reader may want to listen to it: Stravinsky The Rite of Spring // London Symphony Orchestra/Sir Simon Rattle - YouTube)

So imagine that it is the evening of 29 May 1913. You are sitting in the Theatre du Champs-Élysées in Paris, waiting for the curtain to go up. Like everyone else present, you are on tenterhooks, because of the rumors that have been circulating regarding this work. Apparently, it is based on pagan myths, which suggests violence and sexuality. Word also has it that the music would consist of "nothing but primitive banging." The piece opens with a bassoon solo in high register, followed by wind instruments "with twisted chromatic lines and dislocated fragments layered on top of one another." There is a dissonant repeated chord; the dancers jerk like puppets to the beat of it. The audience can't take it; a riot ensues, and it's hard to hear the music. Stravinsky, disgusted by the audience reaction, storms out of the auditorium.(8)

There are numerous conflicting versions of what actually went down. Stravinsky claimed that the whole thing degenerated into "a terrific uproar." The conductor, Pierre Monteux, reported that they had to call in the police. Did members of the audience attack each other, verbally or otherwise? All told, it was a night to remember.(9)

And what of the actual content, beyond the musical score, which many in the audience felt amounted to little more than noise? As noted in Chapter 7, it consists of various primitive rituals celebrating the coming of spring, at the end of which a young girl is chosen to be the sacrificial victim, and dances herself to death. After which, says Jonathan Cross, "the limp body of the sacrificial victim is raised aloft by shamans in bear skins." The purpose of the sacrifice is to ensure the earth's continued fertility. Of course, given the general din, the chaos and pandemonium, it's not clear how much of the story (or music) got through to the audience. But we can appreciate that such a tale would be rather shocking to a Parisian crowd, no matter how sophisticated or avant-garde.(10)

Four questions present themselves at this point. First, what was Stravinsky up to, in the music he composed? If this was innovation, of what did it consist? Second, what were his sources, assuming the score didn't emerge *ex nihilo*? Third, what were the cultural or historical bases of this particular tale? And finally, what was *The Rite*'s legacy? What impact did it have on the music of the rest of the twentieth century, and beyond?

As to Stravinsky's innovations: it helps to remember that Western music, for centuries, operated on a tension/resolution structure, one which European audiences were accustomed to on a somatic level, and had learned to expect. In other words (as discussed in Chapter 4), Western music generates pleasure by setting up a tension—say, providing a melodic line, then going a few notes above it, and then a few notes below it—and then coming back to the original starting point, thus resolving the tension. (This is also true of rock and roll, but not of jazz.) In a word, Stravinsky broke sharply with that format. What he gives us are rhythms that are asymmetric, discordant. Climaxes are built through an accumulation of elements rather than by developmental progression. There is a famous dissonant chord (known as the "Rite chord") that is repeated hundreds of times to generate a timeless sense of ritual. The effect is hypnotic.(11)

Beyond *Rite*, as in *Les Noces* (1923), Stravinsky began to experiment with atonal harmony, along the lines of Schoenberg, Alban Berg, Debussy, and Hindemith. His *Symphony of Psalms* (1930), for example, is similar to Russian Orthodox chanting, where, according to Jonathan Cross, "an egoless state was achieved by the worshipper in focusing not on the meaning of what is being sung but on individual or reiterated syllables." Pleasure is thus derived from the sound itself, which creates a transcendent sense of time—"ontological time." But Stravinsky's chief innovation was his focus on rhythm, the introduction of irregular meters and syncopation. The best explication I have found of this is by the eminent American musicologist and music historian, Richard Taruskin, who said of *The Rite*:

> This highly original composition, with its shifting and audacious rhythms and its unresolved dissonances, was an early modernist landmark… [In it] he presented a new concept of music involving constantly changing rhythms and metric imbalances…and drastically dissonant harmonies that have resonated throughout the 20th century…Working always at the piano, he experimented endlessly with different chord combinations and spacings, explored asymmetrical metrical patterns, and used devices of prolongation and elision to break down the tradition of symmetrical phrasing. Given such sonorities as basic sound objects, rhythm is then regarded as a cumulative process, an

adding together of such into varied groups, as opposed to the varied subdivision of regular groups that forms the basic method of classical music...He had [an] immense influence on the way later composers have felt pulse, rhythm, and form.(12)

Taruskin's scholarship is also relevant to our second question, that of the sources of Stravinsky's innovations, especially since in later years he sought to obscure those sources so as to appear more European. First, Taruskin showed that some of Stravinsky's modernism could be found in Russian music as far back as Mussorgsky; that the discordant harmonies of *The Rite* were not entirely new. But what really blew the lid off the issue of sources was Taruskin's massive two-volume study, *Stravinsky and the Russian Traditions*, which demonstrated in detail that Stravinsky drew more heavily on Russian folk material than had previously been recognized. One source was an anthology of Lithuanian folk melodies that had been collected in the nineteenth century. Whereas Stravinsky later claimed that the opening bassoon solo was the only folk melody he had used, Taruskin was able to show that folk melodies infused the entire score. Despite what was on the surface in Stravinsky's music, said Taruskin, Old Russia remained fundamental to him. As we said earlier, the man's career was defined by the tension between the archaic and the modern, Dionysus and Apollo.(13)

All of this naturally segues into the question of the sources of Stravinsky's stories, i.e., the content of the tales. The pattern here is similar to the sources of his music. For example, the text of *Les Noces* was derived from ethnographic materials that

Stravinsky himself personally collected. In the case of *The Rite*, the hidden story is that it was actually a collaboration with the Russian mystic and expert on folk rituals, Nicholas Roerich. Stravinsky later claimed sole authorship, but this is unlikely. Roerich insisted that it was he, not Stravinsky, who was the source of the story. The scenario is faithful to every detail of Russian midsummer festivals, and Roerich had done extensive research on these sorts of pagan practices. All of this suggests that the tale was based on the latter's knowledge base.(14)

And finally, the legacy. "Enormous" doesn't even begin to capture it. Writing in *The Guardian* in 2023, journalist Sarah Crompton notes that in the 110 years after the premiere of *The Rite,* there have been more than 150 versions of the ballet (some say more than 200). She reviews some of these, starting with Léonide Massine's version of 1920, moving on to Lester Horton's "wild west" version, and then to one by Michael Clark that added music by the Sex Pistols and Stephen Sondheim. Martha Graham created her own version when she was ninety years old. At the present time (2023), there is one by the South African choreographer Dada Masilo, and another by Seeta Patel. In each case, the choreographer provided his or her particular interpretation of Stravinsky's original piece. This includes a marriage version, a flamenco version, and even a climate emergency version. "The far-reaching pull of this masterpiece remains irresistible," she says. More than 100 years later, "it is as vital as ever." Even today, adds Jonathan Cross, young composers are inspired by the score, and Disney used it in the animated film *Fantasia*.(15)

Going beyond *The Rite*, Stravinsky's other works were also very influential. In 1925, Stravinsky partnered up with Georgiy Balanchivadze, more popularly known as George Balanchine, who was twenty-two years his junior. This, says Cross, resulted in "some of the most exciting work ever made for the ballet stage." Balanchine, of course, went on to co-found the New York City Ballet, of which he was the artistic director for more than thirty-five years. In the 1940s Stravinsky wrote a tango for Benny Goodman, along with a concerto; a circus polka for Barnum & Bailey; and ballet scenes for a Broadway revue. His influence extended to Aaron Copland, Leonard Bernstein, Martha Graham, and Steve Reich, among many others.(16)

There is, however, a dark side to the man and his work that cannot be overlooked. As Cross tells it, Stravinsky "had a repellent character." He was deeply anti-Semitic, and believed communism was a Jewish "plague"; and he was often mean, cruel, dishonest, and money-grubbing. He publicly venerated Mussolini, and met with him twice. He stated that he hated liberalism and democracy (let alone any form of socialism), and in the 1960s became a pawn of the US government. This included being showcased at anti-Russian events, as well as dining with Jack and Jackie (who had no interest in his music) at the White House. He became, says Cross, "a piece of priceless Cold War capital."(17)

The attraction to Mussolini and fascism goes along with the Dionysian energy present in *The Rite*. "This is dangerous music," writes Cross, "that taps into the deepest, most primitive instincts." The relation between the avant-garde and fascism is explored in depth by Modris Ecksteins, whom we met in Chapter 7, in his book *Rites of Spring*. The theme of Stravinsky's ballet, he asserts, was birth and death...primitive and violent, the fundamental experiences of all existence, beyond cultural context." "Implicit in the work is an ecstatic turbulence, a thick mélange of instinct, sensuality, and fate." And finally: "Nazism was a popular variant of many of the impulses of the avant-garde. It expressed on a more popular level many of the same tendencies and posited many of the same solutions that the avant-garde did on the level of 'high art'."(18)

The key phrase here is "beyond cultural context," something I explored in an essay on the Italian fascist and Futurist, Filippo Tommaso Marinetti, who was a big fan of Mussolini's as well as of Stravinsky's. The problem with exalting Dionysian energy is that it is context-neutral. It can be adopted by fascism, McCarthyism, or anything else, for virtually any purpose. Appreciating and using this energy is one thing; making a religion out of it is another.(19)

Of course, this in no way diminishes Stravinsky's achievement, which is a permanent fixture in the history of music. But I can't help recalling, years ago, in my Assistant Professor days, having a discussion with an older colleague about history, politics, and the issue of primitive energy. He said something I never forgot: "There are potentially two types of barbarism, rationalism and irrationalism. Either of these, taken straight up, as it were, leads to disaster." I guess Nietzsche had it right all long. (See the epigraph to this book.)

Chapter 9

Bulgakov: The Master and Margarita

For thousands of years the people have used...festive comic images to express their criticism, their deep distrust of official truth, and their highest hopes and aspirations. Freedom was not so much an exterior right as it was the inner content of these images. It was the thousand-year-old language of fearlessness, a language with no reservations and omissions, about the world and about power.

—Mikhail Bakhtin, *Rabelais and His World*

10. Mikhail Bulgakov

Bulgakov: The Master and Margarita

Mikhail Bulgakov (1891-1940) is the writer who most closely follows in the footsteps of Nikolai Gogol. His work, like Gogol's, is clearly a send-up of the governing regime—in his case, the Soviet Union. But there are deeper affinities as well. Like Gogol, Bulgakov sees reality as labile, flexible, full of impossibilities and surprises. (This writing style would later be known as "magical realism.") Also drawing on the Russian folk tradition, his works are filled with witches, vampires, talking cats, and people who can fly. But beyond all that, Bulgakov was fully on board with Gogol's commitment to whimsy. Thus one Internet commentator writes that *"The Master and Margarita* is a reminder that, ultimately, everything is better if you can inject a note of silliness and of the absurd." All dogmas were nonsense, in Bulgakov's eyes, and buffoonery, for him, was an expression of a deep contemplation of life. It is, in fact, a very silly book, and in that, it seems to me, lies its profundity.(1)

Bulgakov wrote the book over the period 1928-40, but a censored version didn't appear until 1966, and an uncensored one until 1973. The crux of his talent, and his satire, was "a skillful blending of fantastic and realistic elements"—once again, Apollo and Dionysus.(2) However, if the stiff, rigid regime of the USSR can be identified with Apollo, then the Dionysian element, which was Bulgakov's response to this (as we also saw in the case of Andrei Bely), had the last laugh. The novel, says one literary critic (echoing Mikhail Bakhtin), "blasts open 'official truths' with the force of a carnival out of control."(3) If it has a plot, it is one that is all over the place. We have (in addition to the witches etc. mentioned above) the activities of demons, a devil's ball, and a meeting of Christ and Pontius Pilate. People miraculously appear and disappear, and a huge black cat tears off someone's head and then replaces it—shades of Gogol. The following paragraph could have easily been written by the author of "The Nose":

> At a huge writing desk with a massive inkstand an empty suit sat and with a dry pen, not dipped in ink, traced on a piece of paper. The suit was wearing a necktie, a fountain pen stuck from its pocket, but above the collar there was neither neck nor head, just as there were no hands sticking out of the sleeves. The suit was immersed in work and completely ignored the turmoil that reigned around it. [The suit, needless to say, can talk.](4)

The second half of the book is almost completely surreal. A group of frogs plays a march on wooden pipes; a cat plays chess with pieces that are alive; polar bears dance, and play concertinas; and at the devil's ball, Margarita comes across a jazz band of apes:

> A huge gorilla with shaggy side-whiskers, a trumpet in his hand, capering heavily, was doing the conducting. Orang-utans sat in a row blowing on shiny trumpets. Perched on their shoulders were merry chimpanzees with concertinas. Two hamadryads with manes like lions played grand pianos, but these grand pianos were not heard amidst the thundering, squeaking and booming of saxophones, fiddles and drums in the paws of gibbons, mandrills and marmosets...Live satin

butterflies bobbed above the heads of the dancing hordes, flowers poured down from the ceiling. In the capitals of the columns, each time the electricity went off, myriads of fireflies lit up, and marsh-lights floated in the air.(5)

When the dust finally settles, toward the end of the story, the Moscow police launch an investigation as to what the heck had happened. They conclude that all of these events hadn't *really* occurred in the real world; rather, they were the work of skilled hypnotists and ventriloquists, who were able to hypnotize large groups of people over great distances. In this way, everything is "explained." Christ and Pilate are reconciled; the Master finishes the novel he was working on, and is reunited with Margarita, his true love. End of story.

Once again, we see the Russian theme of reality not being one fixed thing. In her very imaginative study, *How to Do Nothing*, Jenny Odell writes that "something like collage [Bakhtin's "carnival," perhaps] is at the heart of the unstable and highly personal process of perception." Such perception involves a major shift, which (she says) is "unmooring." Like Alice, we live on the edge of a rabbit hole, and can sometimes fall into it. We don't live strictly Apollonian lives.(6)

With Bulgakov, then, we have the world of Gogol and Bely stretched to the limit, and this is his enduring legacy. The novel is credited with inspiring Salman Rushdie (*The Satanic Verses*), as well as the music of the Rolling Stones ("Sympathy for the Devil"). Numerous films and TV series are based on it, and in 2021 the Bolshoi Theater performed a ballet using the section of the devil's ball. Countries that have produced film versions of the novel include Finland, Poland, Italy, Russia, Iran, Hungary, France, and Israel, and the BBC did it as a radio broadcast in 2015. It has been adapted on stage by more than 500 theater companies, and been the inspiration of more than 250 songs. A number of symphonies are based on it, along with several operas. It has also been the subject of comic strips and graphic novels. In a word, there is something fascinating about this work that has generated and attracted worldwide attention, and continues to do so. We might well ask ourselves why.(7)

This is just a guess on my part, but M&M captures the "collage-like" quality of human life, and the instability/lability of human perception, as very few other novels have done. This is what Bakhtin was talking about: on a fundamental level, despite our "official" behavior and ideologies, we *know* that dogma of any kind is bullshit, and that rejecting it is the road to freedom. It's a fair bet that a century from now, we will still be celebrating the vibrancy, and the iconoclasm, of *The Master and Margarita*.

Chapter 10

Tarkovsky: Solaris

[*2001: A Space Odyssey* is] a lifeless schema with only pretensions to truth.

—Andrei Tarkovsky

[*Solaris* is an] exploration of the unreliability of reality and the power of the human unconscious, [and a] great examination of the limits of rationalism and the perverse power of even the most ill-fated love...

—Salman Rushdie

The Soul of Russia

11. Andrei Tarkovsky

One can't really discuss *Solaris*, Andrei Tarkovsky's film of 1972, without at the same time referring to Stanley Kubrick's film of 1968, *2001: A Space Odyssey*, inasmuch as Tarkovsky admitted that his own film was a response to Kubrick's. This was because he regarded the latter as sterile and superficial—a correct assessment, in my view. Although the general American reaction was to celebrate *2001* as the greatest sci-fi movie ever made, there were a few dissenting voices, which agreed with Tarkovsky's take on it. Pauline Kael of the *New Yorker* called it "monumentally unimaginative," while historian Arthur Schlesinger found it "morally pretentious." Sci-fi writer Ray Bradbury scored it for being banal, while Samuel Delaney pointed out that the characters in the film never say anything meaningful. Meanwhile, someone in the audience in San Francisco ran into the screen, screaming "It's God!", which did approximate the dominant national opinion of the thing.(1)

At this point I must ask the reader's indulgence to draw on my own work on the history of American technology as a preamble to grasping the essential difference between the two films. I believe that this might provide a larger perspective, and thereby allow us to see what a remarkable achievement *Solaris* really is. The essay I am referring to, in particular, is the third chapter of *Why America Failed*, entitled "The Illusion of Progress." I begin with a quote from Martin Luther King: "When scientific power outruns moral power, we end up with guided missiles and misguided men." And a misguided movie —one filled with moral pretensions as opposed to genuine morality—along with an adoring, misguided nation. Let's take a moment, then, to explore the historical context of Kubrick's film.(2)

I don't think we fully realize the huge influence technology has exerted over the American way of life; how integral it has been to the American Dream. A leading philosopher of technology, Albert Borgmann, demonstrated quite convincingly that politics, in America, exists on a metalevel, and that it is the technological order that is the real one. Politics in America is pretty much a smokescreen, and in the absence of genuine politics, substantive politics, technology moves in to fill the vacuum. As such, it acts as a kind of hidden religion, tied to notions of unlimited "progress," and ultimately, salvation (i.e., the answer to all our problems). One of America's greatest historians, Leo Marx, wrote that from the early eighteenth century on, "the awe and reverence once reserved for the Deity...[were] directed toward technology." His student, David Nye, expanded upon this theme in his outstanding study, *American Technological Sublime*. The technological sublime, he says, is the sense of awe or astonishment one might be seized with upon encountering (for example) the Brooklyn Bridge. Thus the artist Joseph Stella wrote how he would stand on the Bridge, feeling as though he was "on the threshold of a new religion or in the presence of a new DIVINITY."(3)

This adoration runs in a continuous thread from the Erie Canal in 1825 to the landing of a man on the moon in 1969—one year after the release of *2001*—and beyond. One movie critic sees Kubrick's film as a pitch for space exploration, and adds that it "shows western expansion as an integral part of [human] evolution." This expansion, which is the American definition of "progress," is the dominant American narrative of what life is all about, and is basically a hamster cage, one that blocks our ability to ask the sort of questions that Tarkovsky was asking in *Solaris*; such as, What is it that makes us human? Personally, I like the Brooklyn Bridge, but I doubt that it can answer that question.(4)

One more digression, before we turn to *Solaris*. Relevant to this discussion is the life of Alan Turing, the father of the modern computer, and the man who pretty much launched the field of Artificial Intelligence. For Turing, literally everything could be reduced to machinery. It was this that enabled him to crack the German Enigma code during World War II, and he extended this approach to the entire world. Turing did have a brief flirtation with spirituality in his early twenties, but soon gave it up for a commitment to materialism and atheism. It was toward the end of his life that he began to feel something primal was missing, and that he had been attempting to fill the void in his life with computers and calculation. Noteworthy, for our purposes, is that Turing's 1950 groundbreaking essay, "Computing Machinery and Intelligence," was the inspiration for *2001*, and that the computer in the movie, called HAL, was based on Turing's ideas. It was thus a bit startling for me to learn that Stanley Kubrick once described HAL as "psychotic," which might tell us something about the nation that adulated the film, considered it profound. Indeed, the film was selected for preservation in the National Film Registry of the Library of Congress, and in 2010 named the greatest film of all time(!) by *The Moving Arts Film Journal*.(5)

In any case, Turing did have something of a spiritual awakening subsequent to his 1950 essay. What was he living for? Was it enough? Was it even human? He began seeing a Jungian analyst, and reading "soul-writers" whose focus was on the inner life, such as Tolstoy and E.M. Forster. It seems like he was finally opening the door to a real life, as opposed to a purely digital one. In his commentary on *2001*, and the computer HAL, the American poet Don Chiasson suggests that there is a bruised heart beating under its mechanized circuitry. And here we have the crucial difference between the two films: whereas *Solaris* is an exploration of that bruised heart, and a meditation on the meaning of life, *2001* is little more than an attempt, via whiz-bang technology, to hide that wound, run away from it.(6)

"There aren't a lot of space battles and laser guns here," says film critic Josh Larsen, commenting on *Solaris*. Tarkovsky's technique is totally different from Kubrick's—slow rather than fast. He employs long, contemplative takes to lull you into a meditative trance. "Especially languorous," says Larsen, "are the full-screen images of Solaris itself, a roiling, misty ocean of a planet that the scientists suspect is a sentient being...." At the end, we are knee-deep in mystery. The film is an exploration of the unknown in us all.(7)

So let's turn to the plot. Kris Kelvin, a psychologist, is having a conversation with a retired pilot named Burton, who tells him about a Soviet space station circling the (fictional) planet Solaris. Strange things have been happening there; Kelvin is charged with investigating. He arrives on Solaris to find one crew member dead by suicide and two more in a very disturbed condition. Pervading the station is an air of the eerie and the paranormal. The planet, as it turns out, is in fact sentient; it has the ability to enter the minds of the cosmonauts and make their memories real. This disorients the crew to the point of insanity. Meanwhile, on the next day, Kelvin is presented with a duplicate of his late wife, Hari, who committed suicide ten years before. Hari cannot be killed; if that occurs, she can simply be replaced. At the end of the story, Kelvin appears to be back on Earth, embracing his father. But the reality(?) is that they are actually on an island on the surface of the sea that covers Solaris.(8)

Most of the drama of the film is a mental one, and it is essentially mystical—spiritual, if not overtly religious. Hari is a phantom, yet no less real for that, and Kelvin loves her, even in a "facsimile" version. In addition, he is completely disoriented, not clear as to what is real. As one critic put it, "memories, love, and life are simply a part of the unknown, unseen, and unheard." Tarkovsky's work, said Ingmar Bergman, "captures life as a reflection, life as a dream."(9)

Who, and what, are we as human beings? When we love someone, who is it that we really love? And love, for Tarkovsky, is finally what it's all about, not technological toys, or the naïve and foolish worship of those toys. At the end of the day, American culture is shallow, little more than a business civilization in decline, to quote economist Robert Heilbroner. We don't have a Pushkin, or a Dostoevsky, or a Stravinsky; what we have is Stanley Kubrick, and an American public that regards his particular version of the technological sublime as the last word in profundity. Let us also recognize that America is an Apollonian culture, in which it has become hard to breathe—a "lifeless schema," per Tarkovsky. The dominant narrative so exalted by Kubrick has proven to be a death sentence. That reality is labile, as Tarkovsky and so many Russian writers and artists have argued, is thus a *good* thing; it has the potential to open doors, point to alternative possibilities.

Tarkovsky died in Paris in 1986, having won numerous awards, and having influenced many filmmakers and millions of filmgoers. His wife, Larisa, had this epitaph engraved on his tombstone: "To the man who saw the Angel." And maybe he did, *mes amis*; maybe he did.

Notes

Preface

1. Caryl Emerson, *The Cambridge Introduction to Russian Literature* (Cambridge: Cambridge University Press, 2008), p. 62.

2. Suzanne Massie, *Land of the Firebird* (New York: Simon & Schuster, 1981), pp. 174 and 179-80.

3. Orlando Figes, *Natasha's Dance* (New York: Picador, 2003), p. 113.

4. Emerson, *Cambridge Introduction*, pp. 170-76. Russian literature, however, has been viewed through a number of "lenses," some more persuasive than others. For an Edward Said-style "colonialist" interpretation, to take just one example, see Elif Batuman, "Novels of Empire," *New Yorker*, 30 January 2023, pp. 42-51.

NOTES

5. Tolstoy did write fairy tales, of course, mostly for children; and in his early days, Dostoevsky showed some interest in the folkloric tradition, as in his novel *The Mistress* (1847). (See studies by George Gibian, Linda Ivanits, and Clint Walker for discussions of this aspect of his work.)

CHAPTER ONE

1. Jeffrey Brooks, *The Firebird and the Fox* (Cambridge: Cambridge University Press, 2019), pp. 2-3; Wikipedia, "Alexander Pushkin"; "Aleksandr Pushkin," www.britannica.com; Suzanne Massie, *Land of the Firebird* (New York: Simon & Schuster, 1981), pp. 204 and 211; gale.com/intl/databases-explored/literature/alexander-pushkin, "Aleksandr Pushkin"; Robert Chandler (ed.), *Russian Magic Tales from Pushkin to Platonov* (New York: Penguin, 2013), p. 5; T.J. Binyon, *Pushkin* (New York: Knopf, 2003), pp. 12 and 89.

2. For the story itself, I used the one included in a collection of Pushkin tales, trans. Alan Myers (Oxford: Oxford University Press, 2009). The story is on pp. 71-100.

3. For an extensive discussion of the various interpretations of the story, see Neil Cornwell (ed.), *Pushkin's* The Queen of Spades (2nd ed.; Bristol: Bristol Classical Press, 2001). Reading this study, one has the impression of being plunged into some variety of medieval Scholasticism. Cornwell refers to the "seemingly endless analysis" of critics of the story, and even seems to poke fun at this modern version of angels dancing on the head of a pin. Thus we have (e.g.) numerological analyses, Freudian analyses, Lacanian analyses, claims for the

influence of Freemasonry, or for the impact of contemporary social change, and so on. "One might," writes Cornwell, "question the necessity for this." Indeed. When you finally have one critic claiming that the story is a huge myth that is meaningful precisely because it has almost no meaning (Cornwell, p. 29), you begin to suspect that a kind of insanity has entered the Pushkin interpretation "industry," in which these commentators are unwittingly or unconsciously duplicating the manic obsession of Hermann in the story.

I hope my own interpretation is not seen as simplistic; it strikes me as being quite plausible, and avoids this dense forest of what Cornwell refers to at one point as "mind-boggling detail." It also suggests ambiguity, which is another school of interpretation (Cornwell, p. 31 and *passim*). In any case, Caryl Emerson worked out a four-part classification scheme for the various approaches that is helpful as a guide; see "'The Queen of Spades' and the Open End," in David Bethea (ed.), *Puškin Today* (Bloomington: Indiana University Press, 1993), p. 34.

4. Binyon, P*ushkin*, p. 430. Cf. Emerson's suggestion that the key word here is *shutka*, joke. (See Emerson in Bethea, cited in the previous note.)

5. Wikipedia, "The Prisoner of the Caucasus"; Ethan Helfrich, "Pushkin and the Caucasus: Literary Images of Russia's Eastern Frontier," *Primary Source*, Vol. V Issue II, pp. 17-24 (https://scholarworks.iu.edu); David Schimmelpenninck van der Oye, *Russian Orientalism* (New Haven: Yale University Press, 2010), pp. 67-70.

Notes

6. See Russian Film: "Кавказская Пленница" - "Kidnapping, Caucasian Style" | Ruslanguage School.

Chapter Two

1. Henri Troyat, *Divided Soul*, trans. Nancy Amphoux (Garden City NY: Doubleday, 1973), pp. 9, 18, 74-75, and 78-79.

2. Ibid., pp. 126 and 436-38; Janko Lavrin, "Nikolay Gogol," www.britannica.com/biography/Nikolay-Gogol. For the story itself, I used the one posted at Gogol_TheNose.pdf (gla.ac.uk). The translator is not indicated.

3. "The Nose by Nikolai Gogol," https://study.com/learn/lesson/the-nose-summary-language-analysis.html.

4. Gary Saul Morson, "Russian literature," www.britannica.com/biography.

Chapter Three

1. Laurence Kelly, *Lermontov* (London: Constable, 1977); Wikipedia, "Mikhail Lermontov"; John Garrard, *Mikhail Lermontov* (Boston: Twayne Publishers, 1982); and T.J. Binyon, *Pushkin* (New York: Knopf, 2003), p. 109.

2. On the following see "My Russia" in *Are We There Yet?* (Brattleboro VT: Echo Point Books & Media, 2017), pp. 151-55.

3. Translation by David Yakobi at Mikhail Lermontov - Выхожу один я на дорогу (Vyhozhu odin ya na dorogu) lyrics + English translation (Version #10) (lyricstranslate.com). Reprinted with permission of the translator.

Notes

4. Kelly, *Lermontov*, p. 39. The poem is on pp. 207-8, but involves an important mistranslation (this by Francis Cornford and Esther Salaman, 1943), which I have corrected above. The translators wrote, "And you will have a Cossack's heart," when the word Lermontov used was not *serdtse*, heart, but *dusha*, soul. Quote from Golovin is in Wikipedia, "Mikhail Lermontov."

5. Kelly, *Lermontov*, pp. 34 and 38.

6. Garrard, *Mikhail Lermontov*, pp. 113-19.

7. Ibid., pp. 123-24 and 145.

Chapter Four

1. The following sketch draws on my discussion of Mussorgsky in my essay "My Russia," cited in the Notes to Chapter 3. Other sources include "Modest Mussorgsky," www.britannica.com, and Caryl Emerson, *The Life of Musorgsky* [sic] (Cambridge: Cambridge University Press, 1999).

2. The Russian Composer, Modest Mussorgsky's Works and Life (galaxymusicnotes.com)

3. As Chuck Berry famously put it in 1956, "Roll Over Beethoven!"

Chapter Five

1. Donald Rayfield, *Anton Chekhov* (New York: Henry Holt, 1997), p. 132; www.sparknotes.com/lit/chekhov/section5/ (SparkNotes). For the full text of this story, which was

published in 1886, see Easter Eve by Anton Chekhov (online-literature.com) (The Literature Network).

2. Rayfield, *Anton Chekhov*, p. 352.

3. Anton Chekhov, *The Comic Stories*, trans. H. Pitcher (London: Andre Deutsch, 1998), pp. 148-53. The version I used can be found online at The Siren, A Story, by Anton Chekhov, THE AMERICAN MERCURY - The Unz Review; translation by Avrahm Yarmolinsky.

4. Leonard Neuger, "What is Chekhovs Siren Whispering to Us? On the Unavoidability of the 'Impossible' Creation of the Humanities," *Wielogłos*, Number 2(12), 2012.

Chapter Six

1. Simon Karlinsky, "The Silver Dove," *New York Times*, 27 October 1974. The translation I used was the one by John Elsworth: London, Pushkin Press, 2nd ed., rev., 2010. One might see Mikhail Bulgakov as a candidate for surpassing Bely (see Chapter 9), but in fact *Petersburg* is a deeply psychological novel, whereas *The Master and Margarita*, with its heavy component of slapstick, is not.

2. Karlinsky, "Silver Dove."

3. Elsworth quoted in the Afterword to the novel (see above, n. 1), p. 568.

4. Michael Buening, "Petersburg by Andrei Bely," www.popmatters.com/107347-petersburg-by-andrei-bely-2496046427.html (PopMatters).

Notes

5.*Petersburg*, pp. 319-20 (see above, n. 1).

Chapter Seven

1.Sjeng Scheijen, *Diaghilev: A Life*, trans. Jane Hedley-Prôle and S.J. Leinbach (New York: Oxford University Press, 2009), pp. 68, 74, and 78.

2.Ibid., pp. 96-98, 101, 106-7, and 112; Wikipedia, "Sergei Diaghilev."

3.Scheijen, *Diaghilev*, p. 90; Wikipedia, "Sergei Diaghilev"; Rupert Christiansen, "How Sergei Diaghilev and the Ballets Russes Revolutionized Dance," https://lithub.com, 19 October 2022 (excerpted from his book *Diaghilev's Empire*); Janet Flanner, "Russian Firebird," *New Yorker*, 5 January 1935; "One art critic": this is from an exhibition on the Ballets Russes held at the Victoria and Albert Museum, 2010-11: "Diaghilev and the Ballets Russes—an Introduction," www.vam.ac.uk. Coco Chanel quoted in "Sergei Diaghilev," www.theartstory.org.

4.Scheijen, *Diaghilev*, p. 1; Ivan Hewett, "The Riot at the Rite," *Telegraph* (London), 25 May 2016; Modris Ecksteins, *Rites of Spring* (Boston: Houghton Mifflin, 1989), p. 32.

5.Wikipedia, "Sergei Diaghilev"; Ecksteins, *Rites of Spring*, p. 23.

6.Scheijen, *Diaghilev*, pp. 166-68.

7.Ibid., pp. 161, 176, and 183.

Notes

8. Ibid., p. 191 and 201-2; www.theartstory.org, "Sergei Diaghilev." See also Suzanne Massie, *Land of the Firebird* (New York: Simon & Schuster, 1981).

9. Scheijen, *Diaghilev*, pp. 222 and 227; "The Color and Magic of Stravinsky's Petrushka," https://thelistenersclub.com.

10. Scheijen, *Diaghilev*, p. 244; Christiansen, "How Sergei Diaghilev and the Ballets Russes Revolutionized Dance"; Ecksteins, *Rites of Spring*, pp. 27-28. Note that Rodin was not the actual author of his review.

11. Scheijen, *Diaghilev*, pp. 264, 270-71, and 438; V&A exhibition cited above in n. 3; Wikipedia, "The Rite of Spring"; Ecksteins, *Rites of Spring*, p. 13. The girl was Maria Piltz, and the drama critic was Carl Van Vechten, writing for the *New York Press*. For an argument that there *was* no riot at this event, see Tom Service, "The Rite of Spring," *The Guardian*, 12 February 2013.

12. Scheijen, *Diaghilev*, pp. 297-98; www.theartstory.org, "Sergei Diaghilev."

13. Scheijen, *Diaghilev*, pp. 305 and 310.

14. Ibid., p. 335; Daniel Levine, "Sergei Diaghilev," https://heavy.com, 31 March 2017.

15. Scheijen, *Diaghilev*, pp. 6-7; www.theartstory.org, "Sergei Diaghilev"; V&A exhibition cited in n. 3 above.

16. Sources for the following portrait: Kathleen Kuiper, "Léon Bakst," www.britannica.com (this, the Wikipedia article, and the Victoria and Albert exhibition article reproduce some marvelous photos of Bakst's costumes and set designs);

Wikipedia, "Léon Bakst"; "Léon Bakst—design for the ballet," www.vam.ac.uk; "Léon Bakst," www.wikiart.org; https://artsandculture.google.com/story/the-collector-of-success-leon-bakst-the-state-tretyakov-gallery/VQUBSXEITyGILA?hl=en; Scheijen, *Diaghilev*, pp. 101, 201-2, 150, 170, and 176; and Marc Chagall, *My Life*, trans. Elisabeth Abbott (Cambridge MA: Da Capo Press, 1994; orig. Russian ed. 1922), pp. 86-92.

17. Léon Bakst, "The Paths of Classicism in Art," trans. Robert Johnson in *Dance Chronicle*, xiii/2 (1990), pp. 170-92; discussed in Jonathan Cross, *Stravinsky* (London: Reaktion Books, 2015), p. 123.

18. Cross, *Stravinsky*, pp. 11-17.

Chapter Eight

1. Wikipedia, "Igor Stravinsky"; Jonathan Cross, *Stravinsky* (London: Reaktion Books, 2015), pp. 147-48.

2. Cross, *Stravinsky*, pp. 26-27.

3. Sjeng Scheijen, *Diaghilev: A Life*, trans. Jane Hedley-Prôle and S.J. Leinbach (New York: Oxford University Press, 2009), p. 312; Tom Service, "The Rite of Spring," *The Guardian*, 12 February 2013; fondation-igor-stravinsky.org; Janet Flanner, "Russian Firebird," *New Yorker*, 5 January 1935.

4. Cross, *Stravinsky*, pp. 31-33.

5. Ibid., pp. 34 and 42-44.

6. Ibid., pp. 34 and 44; Scheijen, *Diaghilev*, pp. 201 and 228.

7. Wikipedia, "Petrushka"; Cross, *Stravinsky*, pp. 44-47.

8. Cross, *Stravinsky*, pp. 48-50.

9. Scheijen, *Diaghilev*, pp. 271-72.

10. Cross, *Stravinsky*, p. 51; Sarah Crompton, "'It's a grief and a healing'," *The Guardian*, 12 February 2023.

11. Cross, *Stravinsky*, pp. 51 and 57.

12. Ibid., pp. 114 and 118; Scheijen, *Diaghilev*, p. 264; Eric Walter White and Richard Taruskin, "Igor Stravinsky," www.britannica.com. Regarding atonality: tonality is the (Western) musical system based on major and minor keys. Atonality means the music is not based on any particular key, so there is no tension and release cycle. No chord "wants" to specially resolve into the next one, in other words. To Western ears, this can be extremely jarring.

13. White and Taruskin, "Igor Stravinsky"; Richard Taruskin, *Stravinsky and the Russian Traditions* (2 vols; Oakland: University of California Press, 1st vol. 1966); Wikipedia, "Richard Taruskin"; Cross, *Stravinsky*, pp. 56, 66, and 87.

14. Cross, *Stravinsky*, pp. 54-55 and 73-74; Crompton, "'It's a grief and a healing'"; Orlando Figes, *Natasha's Dance* (New York: Picador, 2003), p. 279.

15. Crompton, "'It's a grief and a healing'"; Cross, *Stravinsky*, p. 58.

16. Cross, *Stravinsky*, pp. 121, 144, and 190-91.

17. Ibid., pp. 168 and 178-79; Wikipedia, "Igor Stravinsky."

18. Cross, *Stravinsky*, p. 60; Modris Ecksteins, *Rites of Spring* (Boston: Houghton Mifflin, 1989), pp. 39, 52, and 311.

19. Morris Berman, *Genio: The Story of Italian Genius* (Brattleboro VT: Echo Point Books & Media, 2019), Chapter 7. Janet Flanner notes that at the premiere of *Petrushka* in Rome, Marinetti showed up with a banner that said "Down with Wagner, Long Live Stravinsky." See Flanner, "Russian Firebird."

Chapter Nine

1. "One Internet commentator": If you Google "The Master and Margarita," Wikipedia, this comment appears under the question of what the message of the book is. Other references: Boris Fishman (Foreword) and Richard Pevear and Larissa Volokhonsky (Introduction) to the Pevear-Volokhonsky translation of the book, published by Penguin Books in 2016 (updated version). As for the Russian folk tradition, Bulgakov claimed that his mother was a descendant of Tatar hordes.

2. Wikipedia, "Mikhail Bulgakov."

3. Samuel Thomas, "The Master and Margarita," www.britannica.com/topic/The-Master-and-Margarita.

4. *The Master and Margarita* (see above, n. 1), p. 186.

5. Ibid., p. 271.

6. Jenny Odell, *How to Do Nothing* (Brooklyn NY: Melville House, 2019), pp. 99 and 103.

Notes

7. Wikipedia, "Mikhail Bulgakov" and "The Master and Margarita"; Thomas, "The Master and Margarita."

Chapter Ten

1. Wikipedia, "*Solaris*" and "*2001: A Space Odyssey.*" *Solaris* is based on a 1961 novel of the same name by the Polish author Stanisław Lem. However, the point of the book is very different from that of the film, and Lem was very unhappy with the latter when it was released. In brief, the book is interested in the difficulty of communicating with alien life forms, and in speculating about what might constitute alien life, whereas Tarkovsky is exploring our emotional lives, what it means to be human, and the limits of rationality.

2. Morris Berman, *Why America Failed* (Charleston SC: Create Space, 2014; orig. publ. John Wiley & Sons, 2011), Chapter 3.

3. Ibid., pp. 71 and 75-80. Marx taught at MIT. His most celebrated work is *The Machine in the Garden: Technology and the Pastoral Ideal in America.*

4. Berman, *Why America Failed*, p. 80, and Aryaman Kumar, "Solaris 1972 Explained," https://www.cinemamonogatari.com, 21 October 2021.

5. Morris Berman, *Eminent Post-Victorians* (Independent publishing, 2022), Chapter 10; Wikipedia, "2001: A Space Odyssey."

6. Berman, *Eminent Post-Victorians*, Chapter 10.

7. "Solaris," www.larsenonfilm, and Kumar, "Solaris 1972 Explained."

8. Wikipedia, "Solaris"; Roger Ebert, "Solaris," www.rogerebert.com, 19 January 2003; Kumar, "Solaris 1972 Explained"; and "Solaris," https://sites.google.com/site/independentstudyinfilm/solaris-1972.

9. "Solaris," https://sites.google.com/site/independentstudyinfilm/solaris-1972; Wikipedia, "Andrei Tarkovsky."

About the Author

Morris Berman is a poet, novelist, essayist, social critic, and cultural historian. He has written nineteen books and nearly 200 articles, and has taught at a number of universities in Europe, North America, and Mexico. He won the Governor's Writers Award for Washington State in 1990, and was the first recipient of the annual Rollo May Center Grant for Humanistic Studies in 1992. In 2000, *The Twilight of American Culture* was named a "Notable Book" by the *New York Times Book Review*, and in 2013 he received the Neil Postman Award for Career Achievement in Public Intellectual Activity from the Media Ecology Association. Dr. Berman lives in Mexico.